STUDY GUIDE TO ACCOMPANY

Human Resources Management in the Hospitality Industry

David K. Hayes, Ph.D.

Jack D. Ninemeier, Ph.D.

WILEY

JOHN WILEY and SONS, INC.

Library of Congress Cataloging-in-Publication Data:

ISBN 13: 978-0-470-14060-4

Printed in the United States of America

10   9   8   7   6   5   4   3   2   1

TABLE OF CONTENTS

To the Student

In every segment of the hospitality industry, finding, training and retaining outstanding staff members is always a challenging task; but it is one that every manager must master. Your textbook, *Human Resources Management in the Hospitality Industry* has been developed to help you master that challenge.

As the authors identified the content for this hospitality-specific HR text, they recognized the distinction between HR Management and Supervision. Historically, many hospitality students have been taught how to "supervise" employees. The reasoning was simple: "good" managers become recognized as such by first being good "supervisors." In today's litigious society, however, managers (and those students who will become managers) who do not understand the legal requirements and other responsibilities that must underpin their actions are greatly disadvantaged. *Human Resources Management in the Hospitality Industry* was designed to give you the *advantage* of knowing the legal obligations, responsibilities, and management skills necessary to succeed in managing human resources.

This *Student Guide to Human Resources Management in the Hospitality Industry* will help you in learning and reviewing the important information you will find in the text. It is organized with 13 sections; one for each text chapter. Each study guide section provides you the following learning tools:

- *Learning Objectives Review*
- *Study Notes*
- *Boxed Key Terms*
- *Key Terms & Concept Review*
- *Practice Quiz*
- *For Your Consideration*

The *Learning Objectives Review* re-states the learning goals of each chapter. They are identical to those found in the text. The *Study Notes* are intended to help you better understand key points and concepts found in the text. They serve as a chapter outline and emphasize important text statements. The *Key Terms* included in this study guide have been boxed for easy recognition. They provide definitions for many of the terms you should know when you finish reading the chapters.

The *Key Terms and Concept Reviews* have been designed to help you test your understanding of each key term identified in its respective chapter. The *Practice Quizzes* have also been developed to help you test your knowledge of critical chapter information. Taking them can help you prepare for exams you may be given by your own class instructor. When you have completed the quizzes, be sure to check your scores. You can do so because the answers to each *Key Terms & Concepts Quiz* as well as each *Practice Quiz* are located at the end of each section. Each chapter concludes with a *For Your Consideration* open-ended question to encourage you to think conceptually about human resources topics.

David K. Hayes   Jack D. Ninemeier

Chapter 1
Introduction to Human Resources in the Hospitality Industry

Learning Objectives Review

At the conclusion of this chapter, you will be able to:

1. Provide a brief overview of the hospitality and tourism industries, and emphasize the importance of effective human resources management to all organizations within them.

2. Explain how human resources management relates to the management of a hospitality and tourism organization.

3. Present an overview of human resources activities, and explain external and internal influences that affect them.

4. Review the importance of diversity in the hospitality workplace, and tell basic procedures important in planning and implementing a valuing-diversity emphasis.

5. List specific human resources responsibilities important in most hospitality and tourism organizations.

Study Notes

The following summary includes many of the important points found in this chapter. Key terms are boxed for easy recognition.

1. Overview of Hospitality Industry

- The hospitality industry has often been described as a "people business."

- The hospitality industry is one part of the larger travel and tourism industry that, in addition to hospitality, consists of transportation services organizations and retail businesses.

- The for-profit and not-for-profit operations in the hospitality segment share a common goal: to provide lodging and/or accommodations including food services for people when they are away from their homes.

- Organizations in the hospitality industry tend to be labor-intensive.

> **Labor-intensive**: The situation in which people rather than technology and equipment are used to provide products and services for an organization's consumers.

> **Human resources (HR)**: The persons employed by a hospitality or tourism organization.

> **Intrapreneur**: An employee of an organization whose compensation, in whole or in part, is based on the financial performance of the part of the business for which the person is responsible.

2. Managing Human Resources in the organization

- The staff members of every hospitality and tourism organization are its most important resource

Management Function	Level of Management		
	Top-Level Manager	Mid-Level Manager	Supervisor
Planning	Analyzes the number of persons needed for key management positions in the future (succession planning).	Considers estimated costs of departmental training programs for an upcoming budget period.	Schedules employees for the following week.
Organizing	Determines reporting relationships as a hotel front office department is reorganized.	Determines tasks to be part of a specific position.	Revises a work task based on work simplification tactics.
Staffing	Recruits and hires employees for a healthcare dietary services operation.	Provides input about a hire or fire decision.	Provides input to job descriptions used for employee recruitment.
Supervising	Directs the work of managers.	Directs the work of supervisors.	Directs the work of entry-level employees.
Controlling	Establishes labor standards for a quick-service restaurant.	Compares estimated and actual labor cost data, and takes corrective actions as necessary.	Ensures that procedures used to control costs are in use.
Appraising	Determines the extent to which human resources goals, including labor costs, professional development programs, and performance improvement, are met.	Evaluates the work of department staff.	Determines whether revised work procedures that address a problem have corrected it.

> **Resources**: What an organization has available to achieve goals. Examples include people (human resources), money, time, machinery, processes and procedures, energy (utilities), and products such as food, beverages, and supplies.

- Top-level managers tend to have longer-term, big-picture responsibilities, managers have more specific departmental-related duties, and supervisors serve as linking pins to connect upper levels of management with entry-level staff members in day-to-day operations.

> **Managers**: Staff members in the organization who direct the work of supervisors.

> **Supervisors**: Staff members in the organization who direct the work of entry-level personnel.

- Numerous federal and state laws relating to hiring and employment practices must be understood and implemented in every hospitality and tourism organization. The extent of compliance has a significant impact on how affected managers make personnel-related decisions and on whether significant time and financial resources must be committed to issues that could have been avoided if labor laws were followed.

- Those with human resources responsibilities are at the forefront of helping to develop, implement, communicate, interpret, and enforce the policies and procedures that help ensure that the organization's most important resources (employees) are empowered to help the organization achieve its goals.

> **Corporate culture**: Shared beliefs, experiences, and norms that influence how things are done within an organization

- Labor shortages are an ongoing challenge, and much of a manager's time is often spent in recruiting and training new employees and in correcting defects caused by employees who don't care before they resign and by newly hired personnel who are concerned, but who have not completed training in proper work procedures.

- Reasons for labor shortages vary by location but typically include an inadequate number of persons desiring to work in the industry, perceived low compensation, and, unfortunately, very high employee turnover rates.

- Managers can use three basic strategies to address labor shortages, and each has human resources implications:

1. Keep the people currently employed; reduce the turnover rate. Selecting the right people and using tactics to retain staff members are examples of ways to accomplish this goal.

2. Increase productivity. When increased output that meets required standards is generated with the same or reduced number of labor hours, fewer personnel will be needed. Again, selecting the right persons is helpful, as is providing well-thought-out orientation, training, and professional development programs for interested staff members.

3. Recruit from nontraditional labor markets. Many hospitality and tourism managers enjoy great success when they employ "empty nesters" (parents of grown children), older workers seeking part-time employment to complement retirement income, and other persons with physical and mental challenges who can become proficient at performing many necessary tasks.

> **Employee turnover**: The proportion of total employees replaced during a specific time period. For example, the annual turnover rate can be calculated as the number of employees leaving during a year divided by the number of employees in the workforce.

3. Human Resource Activities: External Influences and Internal Influences

> **Human resources department**: The department within a large hospitality or tourism organization with the responsibility for recruiting, screening, and developing staff members. Persons in this department also administer compensation and benefit programs, coordinate safety practices, implement labor law requirements, and, if applicable, administer collective bargaining agreements.

Activities

- *Recruiting/selecting.* These tasks include tactics and procedures to attract applicants to the organization (recruiting) and choosing the very best persons among them (selecting).

- *Training and development.* Preparing new staff members to do required work, updating their experienced peers, and providing opportunities for all interested staff members to assume more responsible positions are integral to the efforts of most organizations to attain goals and address competitive pressures, if applicable.

- *Compensation and appraisal.* Personnel should receive pay and benefits commensurate with their contributions to the organization. Performance appraisal provides input to help

- *Protection and communications.* Safety and security concerns are of obvious importance to all employees. Many laws and regulations mandate safety procedures, and numerous other tactics that top-level managers should do (and not do) impact employee safety. Many legal and procedural issues with safety implications are addressed by those with human resources responsibilities. These topics are discussed in Chapter 10. In addition, effective communication that flows up, down, and across the organization helps ensure that staff members know about issues that affect them.

Staff specialists: Persons with technical expertise in an area such as human resources that provide advice to, but do not make decisions for, managers in the organization's chain of command.

External Influences

- *Legislation.* The impact of federal, state, and other laws on the hiring process and their influence on management decisions affecting personnel cannot be overstated.

- *Consumer preferences.* What consumers desire must be identified and supplied by hospitality and tourism organizations. What are business/operating volumes? What products and services must be produced, and when are they needed? The answers to these and related questions drive employee recruiting and selecting, training and development, and compensation and appraisal activities.

- *Demographics.* The characteristics of the local labor market and the guests are of obvious concern. Income levels in a community affect wage and salary rates, and they also impact the ability and interest of consumers to purchase the organization' products and services. Young persons are the foundation of employees in many organizations; are they available?

- *Global issues.* Many hospitality and tourism organizations exist to serve travelers. Business volumes impact human resources activities, and these are affected by international and national events that encourage (e.g., sporting events and special commemorations) and discourage (e.g., violence and disease threats) travel.

- *Economy.* The financial well-being of world markets and the country, state, and community in which the hospitality organization operates impact business volumes and, therefore, the need for human resources.

- *Employee unions.* Staff members may belong to an employee union that represents their interests in numerous aspects of the human resources activities noted in Figure 1.3.

> **Employee union**: An organization of employees who act together to protect and promote their interests by collective bargaining with representatives of the hospitality and tourism organization.

Internal Influences

- *Policies*. A policy can greatly influence how an organization feels about staff members. In the absence of laws that regulate specific actions, employers have significant discretion in establishing protocols that may affect the attitudes of staff members toward the organization.

- *Work Procedures*. Work procedures that are designed with (or without) input from applicable personnel, the extent to which equipment is used to ease physical work tasks and the amount of employee *empowerment*, if any, impact how work is done and, in turn, required human resources activities.

- *Corporate culture*. The perceived worth of employees to the organization is an integral part of its culture. It drives the philosophies and attitudes about employees and their roles in the organization, and human resources activities.

- *Long- and short-term plans*. Longer-term plans such as expansion or *downsizing* and shorter-term plans such as rolling out a new program or service impact employees and affect recruiting, selecting, and training activities.

- *Management judgment and experience*. Managers and human resources specialists (in large organizations) bring their own judgment and experience to the decision-making process. This input affects the policies, procedures, and plans already discussed and influences other decisions about human resources issues.

> **Policy**: Rules and regulations established by an organization that specify how applicable staff members should act.

> **Work procedure**: A course of action or steps to be used to accomplish an objective; usually developed to describe how a work task should be accomplished.

> **Empowerment**: The act of authorizing employees to make discretionary decisions within their areas of responsibility.

> **Downsizing**: Activities implemented to eliminate jobs in order to generate greater efficiencies and cost savings.

4. Diversity in the Hospitality Workplace

Overview of Diversity

Diversity: The broad range of human characteristics and dimensions that impact the employees' values, opportunities, and perceptions of themselves and others at work.

- A reasonable definition of diversity might separate the entire population into the six characteristics noted earlier: age, gender, mental/physical abilities, sexual orientation, race, and ethnic heritage. These factors do influence how one experiences the world; however, numerous secondary dimensions also shape one's values, expectations, and experiences. These include education, family status, organizational role and level, religion, first language, income, geographic location, and numerous others.

Equal Employment Opportunity Laws and Affirmative Action Programs Are Different from Valuing-Diversity Efforts

- A welcoming and rewarding work environment encourages excellent job performance.

- The changing makeup of the U.S. labor force increasingly requires the employment of those with diverse personal dimensions.

- When all employees are valued, turnover and absenteeism are minimized and associated costs are reduced.

- A culture of understanding, respect, and cooperation encourages teamwork with its benefits.

- Diverse backgrounds create more creative alternatives as decisions are made and as problems are resolved.

- Many consumers are attracted to businesses that employ staff members who reflect the diversity of those consumers. The result is increased sales volume, which, in turn, improves the financial viability of the organization.

Implementing Diversity Initiatives

- Valuing diversity requires a change in corporate culture, and these change efforts never end.

- When diversity is valued, benefits accrue to employees and to the organization.

- Efforts to implement diversity efforts should include everyone, because every staff member brings diverse attitudes, backgrounds, and experiences to the job.

Group members have a formidable task in most organizations. They must:

- Obtain input from numerous internal and external sources.

- Identify and consider cultural diversity implementation concerns.

- Arrive at objective conclusions about the readiness of the organization to adapt to cultural change.

- Develop specific and useful plans.

- Assign tasks and monitor their completion.

- Communicate effectively with leaders about diversity issues.

- Plan ongoing activities that promote diversity and its benefits to the organization's staff members.

Diversity goals recognize simple issues. Those who support the concept believe that all staff members want to:

- Be recognized for whom they are and appreciated for what they do.

- Feel comfortable with whom they work.

- Believe that their input is valued and that they have some impact on the decisions that affect them.

Those with human resources responsibilities must stay current with applicable laws, must interpret and apply them correctly, and must be able to communicate their organizations' positions about all matters, including compensation, that affect their employees.

5. Specific Human Resource Responsibilities

The following section outlines some of the specific responsibilities of a Human resource department.

Most hospitality and tourism organizations are too small to enjoy the services of one or more human resources specialists. In that case, managers have only a few options available:

- The general manager must assume responsibility for some of these tasks.

- A decentralized approach may be used in which department heads are responsible for the personnel-related issues relevant to their specific staff.

- Basic policies and procedures are implemented, and a qualified attorney is contacted when issues arise that appear to be outside the boundaries that they impose.

- Unfortunately, other tasks may not be accomplished or may be done incorrectly.

- Most hospitality and tourism organizations are too small to enjoy the services of one or more human resources specialists. In that case, managers have only a few options available:

- The goal of managers in small operations should be to address the most important topics likely to cause the most significant problems.

Executive committee: A group comprising department heads who serve as the organization's key management team and who, in this capacity, are responsible for the overall management of the organization.

Key Terms & Concepts Review: Quiz #1

This key terms and concepts quiz is designed to help you learn and better understand important chapter concepts and improve your Human Resources-related vocabulary.

Match the key terms with their correct definitions.

1. Corporate culture _____

2. Diversity _____

3. Downsizing _____

4. Employee turnover _____

5. Employee union _____

6. Empowerment _____

7. Executive committee _____

8. Hospitality industry _____

9. Human resources _____

10. Human resources department _____

11. Human resources management _____

a. The broad range of human characteristics and dimensions that impact the employees' values, opportunities, and perceptions of themselves and others at work.

b. Shared beliefs, experiences, and norms that influence how things are done within an organization.

c. Processes used by a hospitality or tourism organization to enhance its performance by effectively using all of its staff members.

d. The department within a large hospitality or tour-ism organization with the responsibility for recruiting, screening, and developing staff members.

e. The range of for-profit and not-for-profit organizations that provide lodging and/or accommodations including food services for people when they are away from their homes.

f. Activities implemented to eliminate jobs in order to generate greater efficiencies and cost savings.

g. The persons employed by a hospitality or tourism organization

h. The act of authorizing employees to make discretionary decisions within their areas of responsibility.

i. A group comprising department heads who serve as the organization's key management team and who, in this capacity, are responsible for the overall management of the organization.

j. The proportion of total employees replaced during a specific time period.

k. An organization of employees who act together to protect and promote their interests by collective bargaining with representatives of the hospitality and tourism organization.

Key Terms & Concepts Review: Quiz #2

This key terms and concepts quiz is designed to help you learn and better understand important chapter concepts and improve your Human Resources-related vocabulary.

Match the key terms with their correct definitions.

1. Intrapreneur _____

    a. The situation in which people rather than technology and equipment are used to provide products and services for an organization's consumers
        .

2. Job descriptions _____

    b. A list of tasks that a person working within a specific position must perform.

3. Labor-intensive _____

    c. An employee of an organization whose compensation, in whole or in part, is based on the financial performance of the part of the business for which the person is responsible.

4. Management process _____

    d. A course of action or steps to be used to accomplish an objective; usually developed to describe how a work task should be accomplished.

5. Manager _____

    e. The concept that the benefits of money spent on something are worth more to an organization than the amount of money that is spent on its purchase.

6. Policy _____

    f. The amount of money generated from the sale of products and services to consumers of the hospitality operation.

7. Resources _____

    g. Staff members in the organization who direct the work of entry-level personnel.

8. Work procedure _____

    h. Persons with technical expertise in an area such as human resources that provide advice to, but do not make decisions for, managers in the organization's chain of command.

9. Revenue _____

i. Rules and regulations established by an organization that specify how applicable staff members should act.

10. Staff specialists _____

j. What an organization has available to achieve goals

11. Supervisor _____

k. The process of planning, organizing, staffing, supervising, controlling, and appraising organizational resources to attain goals.

12. Value-added _____

l. Staff members in the organization who direct the work of supervisors.

Practice Quiz

To help you test your mastery of the chapter's content, choose the letter of the best answer to each of the questions listed below.

1. The hospitality industry is often described as a:
    A. Hotel and Restaurant Business
    B. People Business
    C. Revenue Maximizing Business
    D. Human Resources Business
Page 4

2. An employee's attitude about their job is most likely to be affected by:
    A. Their benefits package
    B. Their interactions with co-workers and managers
    C. The business' profit margins
    D. The business' level of technological advancement
Page 7

3. The following is NOT a primary human resources activity?
    A. Training and Developing
    B. Protection and Communications
    C. Compensation and Appraisal
    D. Sanitation activities
Pages 11-12

4. Of the following, which is an internal influence on human resources departments?
    A. Corporate Culture
    B. Protection and Communication
    C. Employee Unions
    D. Demographics
Page 14

5. The following is NOT an example of a lodging organization in the hospitality industry?
    A. Inns
    B. Camp and Park Grounds
    C. Health Care Institutions
    D. Destination Resorts
Page 4

6. An example of a *not-for-profit* food service segment would be:
    A. Correctional Facilities
    B. Grocery Stores
    C. Service Stations
    D. Caterers
Page 5

7. A factor that may cause Labor Shortages is:
    A. Unemployment rates rise
    B. Perceived high compensation
    C. Employee turnover rates are high
    D. People make to much money
Page 10

8. The following is NOT likely to be considered a Human Resources Responsibility?
    A. Management of benefit programs
    B. Administration of payroll records
    C. Administration of guest room inspections
    D. Planning recruitment strategies
Page 20

9. Which of the following is NOT considered to be part if the hospitality industry?
    A. Retail Businesses
    B. Strip Malls
    C. Foodservice
    D. Transportation
Page 5

10. The idea of an employee becoming an intrapenuer is intended to:
    A. Help maximize job-sharing
    B. Focus efforts on internal job recruitment
    C. Help parents save for their children's college
    D. Motivate employees by offering profit-sharing plans to staff
Page 6

For Your Consideration

Many HR managers believe that the greatest challenge to developing an effective and diverse work force in the hospitality industry comes not in the melding of worker's of various races, religion and gender, but rather it is the blending of workers from various age groups. Why do you believe this could be the case?

Chapter 2
The Legal Environment of Human Resources Management

Learning Objectives Review

At the conclusion of this chapter, you will be able to:

1. Define and describe "employment law," the legislation directly addressing employer–employee relations.

2. Recognize the importance of the government's role in establishing legal requirements affecting HR management.

3. List and briefly describe selected labor-related legislation enacted in the United States by the federal government.

4. Identify the unique issues facing hospitality companies that operate units in countries with legal systems different from that of the United States.

5. Recognize and appreciate the unique HR-related responsibilities of the hospitality unit manager.

Study Notes

The following is composed of important points from each chapter. Key terms are located in boxes for easy recognition.

1. Employment Law

- Hospitality managers responsible for HR management must fully understand that the wrong HR decision can subject their companies (and themselves!) to significant legal liability.

> **Employment law**: The body of laws, administrative rulings, and precedents that addresses the legal rights of workers and their employers.

- Hospitality managers at all levels should take great care to ensure that their actions do not inadvertently create legal issues for themselves and their companies.

- It is far better for hospitality managers to understand the laws that relate to HR management than to expose their organizations to the fines and litigation that can result from violations of the law.

- Employment law in the United States arose, in most cases, as a result of the demands of workers for better working conditions and the right to organize.

- A hospitality manager must be keenly aware of the individual employment laws that directly affect them, their operation, and their employees.

2. The Government's Role in the Management of Human Resources

- Hospitality managers interact with governmental entities in a variety of different ways, and they must observe the procedures and regulations established by the government. Managers must fill out forms and paperwork, obtain operating licenses, maintain their property to specified codes and standards, provide a safe working environment, and, when required, even open their facilities for periodic inspections.

- Just as the federal government has played and will continue to play an important regulatory role in the hospitality industry, so too do the various state governments.

- Generally, each state regulates significant parts of the employee–employer relationship occurring within its borders. Items such as worker-related unemployment compensation benefits, worker safety issues, and at-work injury compensation fall to the state entity charged with regulating the workplace. In addition, in most states, this entity will also be responsible for areas such as employment assistance programs for both employees and employers.

> **Unemployment compensation**: A benefit paid to an employee who involuntarily loses his or her employment without just cause.

> **Garnish (ment)**: A court-ordered method of debt collection in which a portion of a worker's income is paid directly to one or more of that worker's creditors.

- Most hospitality professionals would agree that all workers are best protected when employers, employees, and governmental entities work together to protect wages, benefits, pensions, safety, and health.

3. A Manager's Review of Significant Employment Legislation

    a. The Civil Rights Act of 1964 (Title VII)

    b. The Age Discrimination in Employment Act of 1967

    c. The Pregnancy Discrimination Act of 1978

    d. The Worker Adjustment and Retraining Notification Act of 1989

    e. The Americans with Disabilities Act (ADA) of 1990

    f. The Family Medical Leave Act of 1993

- Several important pieces of legislation were passed in the very early 1900s. One of the most noteworthy was the Clayton Act of 1914, which legitimized and protected workers' rights to join labor unions.

Labor union: An organization that acts on behalf of its members to negotiate with management about the wages, hours, and other terms and conditions of the membership's employment.

- The Norris-LaGuardia Act, passed in 1932, was the first in a series of laws passed by Congress in the 1930s that gave federal sanction to the right of labor unions to organize and strike.
- Perhaps the most important labor legislation of the 1930s was the National Labor Relations Act (NLRA) of 1935, more popularly known as the Wagner Act, after its sponsor, Sen. Robert F. Wagner (NY-D).

a. The Civil Rights Act of 1964 (Title VII)

- This Civil Rights Act of 1964 contains several sections, but for hospitality employers, the most important of these is Title VII. Title VII of the Civil Rights Act of 1964 outlaws discrimination in employment in any business on the basis of race, color, religion, sex, or national origin. Title VII also prohibits retaliation against employees who oppose such unlawful discrimination.

Title VII: The specific section of the Civil Rights Act of 1964 that outlaws discrimination in employment in any business on the basis of race, color, religion, sex, or national origin.

- In 1972, the passage of the Equal Employment Opportunity Act, a revision to the Civil Rights Act of 1964, resulted in the formation of the Equal Employment Opportunity Commission

> **Equal Employment Opportunity Commission (EEOC):** The entity within the federal government assigned to enforcing the provisions of Title VII of the Civil Rights Act of 1964.

- The following general areas fall under the enforcement jurisdiction of the EEOC:
  1. Race/color discrimination
  2. Age discrimination
  3. National origin discrimination
  4. Pregnancy discrimination
  5. Religious discrimination
  6. Portions of the Americans with Disabilities Act
  7. Sexual harassment

- Title VII prohibits employers from discriminating against individuals because of their religious beliefs when hiring and firing. It also requires employers to, when possible; accommodate the religious practices of an employee or prospective employee, unless doing so would create an undue hardship on the employer.

- In the late 1970s, courts began holding that sexual harassment is also prohibited under the Act, and in 1986, the Supreme Court held in a lawsuit (Meritor *Savings Bank* v. *Vinson*, 477 U.S. 57 (1986)) that sexual harassment is sex discrimination, and thus is prohibited by Title VII.

> **Sexual Harassment:** Unwelcome sexual advances, requests for sexual favors, and other verbal or physical conduct of a sexual nature.

- Affirmative action constitutes a good-faith effort by employees to address past and/or present discrimination through a variety of specific, results-oriented procedures.

- The goal of most affirmative action programs is to broaden the pool of candidates and encourage hiring based on sound, job-related criteria. The intended result is a workforce with greater diversity and potential for all.

> - **Bona fide occupational qualification (BFOQ):** A specific job requirement for a particular position that is reasonably necessary to the normal operation of a business, and thus allowing discrimination against a protected class

- It is important for hospitality managers to understand that, in the general case, federal (as well as many state and local) laws are intended to define and prevent inappropriate disparate treatment *of* employees based on a non-job-related characteristic.

> **Disparate treatment**: The claim that, in the same situation, one employee was treated differently than other employees.

- Disparate treatment is a basic concept in employment discrimination cases. Lawyers classify employment discrimination cases as either disparate treatment cases or disparate (adverse) impact cases.

- In a disparate treatment case, the employee's claim is that the employer treated him or her differently than other employees who were in a similar situation

- Disparate impact policies are illegal and point to the importance of HR managers carefully reviewing all employment policies to ensure they do not inadvertently lead to charges of disparate treatment or disparate impact.

b. The Age Discrimination in Employment Act of 1967

- The Age Discrimination in Employment Act of 1967 (ADEA) was initially passed to prevent the widespread practice (at that time) of requiring employees to retire at age 65.

- The ADEA originally gave protected-group status to those workers between the ages of 39 and 65.

- In 1986, an important amendment to the Age Discrimination in Employment Act eliminated the mandatory retirement age.

- The ADEA makes it unlawful to include age preferences, limitations, or specifications in job notices or advertisements. As a narrow exception to that general rule, a job notice or advertisement may specify an age limit in the rare circumstances where age is shown to be a bona fide occupational qualification (BFOQ) reasonably necessary to the operation of the business.

c. The Pregnancy Discrimination Act of 1978

- Discrimination on the basis of pregnancy, childbirth, or related medical conditions now constitutes unlawful sex discrimination under Title VII. Women affected by pregnancy or related conditions must be treated in the same way as other applicants or employees with similar abilities or limitations.

- An employer cannot refuse to hire a woman because of her pregnancy-related condition as long as she is able to perform the major functions of her job. Also, an employer cannot refuse to hire her because of prejudices against pregnant workers or the prejudices of coworkers, clients, or customers.

d. The Worker Adjustment and Retraining Notification (WARN) Act of 1989

- WARN offers protection to workers by requiring employers to provide notice 60 days in advance of the closing of an employment site or in the event of a mass layoff.

- In the hospitality industry, many restaurants are too small to be covered by WARN. In many cases, limited-service hotels also employ too few workers to be covered. An exception, however, is common in the case of the sale of larger full-service hotels.

Franchisor: The business entity that has sold or granted a franchise.

- "Employment loss" as defined by the WARN Act includes:
  1. Termination, other than a discharge for cause, voluntary departure, or retirement
  2. A layoff exceeding six months
  3. A reduction in an employee's hours of work of more than 50 percent in each month of any six-month period

- An employer who violates the WARN provisions by ordering an employment site closing or a mass layoff without providing appropriate notice is liable to each affected employee for an amount including back pay and benefits for the period of violation (up to 60 days).

e. The Americans with Disabilities Act (ADA) of 1990

- The ADA prohibits discrimination against people with disabilities in the areas of public accommodations, transportation, telecommunications, and employment.

- Three different groups of individuals are protected under the ADA:
  1. An individual with a physical or mental impairment that substantially limits a major life activity. Some examples of what constitutes a "major life activity" under the Act are seeing, hearing, talking, walking, reading, learning, breathing, taking care of oneself, lifting, sitting, and standing.
  2. A person who has a record of a disability
  3. A person who is "regarded as" having a disability

Reasonable accommodation: Any modification or adjustment to a job or the work environment that will enable a qualified applicant or employee with a disability to participate in the application process or to perform the job's essential functions.

- Even with the passage of the ADA, an employer does not have to hire a disabled applicant who is not qualified to do a job. The employer can still select the most qualified candidate, provided that no applicant was eliminated from consideration because of a qualified disability.

f. The Family Medical Leave Act of 1993

- The Family and Medical Leave Act (FMLA) was enacted in February 1993. This law allows an employee to take unpaid leave due to pregnancy, illness, or to care for a sick family member.

- Understanding the FMLA is important for at least two reasons: (1) the actual content and impact of the law; and (2) the history of the FMLA provides managers with a recent (and continuing) example of how employment laws in the United States are proposed, debated in the public arena, and, in many cases, enacted in some form or another.

- In most cases (there are some very limited exceptions for extremely critical or key positions), an employer must allow the employee to return to the same position he or she held when the leave commenced, to an equivalent position, or to one virtually identical to the employee's former position in terms of pay and working conditions, including status and benefits.

4. The International Legal Environment for Multinational Hospitality Companies

- As a hospitality company expands, first with single operations (and, perhaps, franchise partners) in other countries to multiunit management on multiple continents, the legal environment in which that company must operate will become increasingly complex.

- Many hospitality professionals work at some point in their careers with a company that does business internationally. There are a variety of reasons why you might be assigned the responsibility of HR management in your company's international operations. These include:
  1. Your education and past work history give you the experience you need to succeed in the job.
  2. No local staff (in the foreign country) is currently qualified to assume the responsibility.
  3. Your responsibilities include the training of local HR staff.
  4. Local persons are being trained for positions that will ultimately replace the need for your assistance, but they are not yet qualified to assume 100 percent responsibility.

5. Your employer wants you and other managers to gain a global perspective.
6. It is in the company's best long-term interest to improve the cultural understanding between managers and employees in the company's various international components.
7. An international assignment is considered an integral part of your professional development process.
8. There is an interest in obtaining tighter administrative control over a foreign division or addressing and correcting a significant problem.
9. There are HR operating or public relations issues that require long-term on-site management direction to properly address the issues.
10. There is an interest in obtaining tighter administrative control over a foreign division or addressing and correcting a significant problem.
11. There are HR operating or public relations issues that require long-term on-site management direction to properly address the issues.

Expatriate manager: A citizen of one country who is a working manager in another country.

---

5. The Special Role of the Hospitality Unit Manager

- Regardless of whether a hospitality manager's assignment is within his or her own country or outside its borders, unit managers are perhaps the single most important factor affecting an operation's short- and long-term profitability and success.

Unit manager: The individual with the final on-site decision-making authority at an individual hospitality operation.

- Hospitality managers are in charge of securing raw materials, producing a product or service, and selling it—all under the same roof. This makes them very different from their manufacturing counterparts (who are in charge of product production only) and their retail counterparts (who sell, but do not manufacture, the product).

- Hospitality industry journals and publications (many of them delivered online) can be of real assistance in helping you follow legislation at the national level. Reading about the hospitality industry will not only make you a better unit manager, but will let you keep up with changing regulations as well.

- As a hospitality manager, it is important for you to stay involved in the hospitality trade association that most closely represents your industry segment. The National Restaurant Association (NRA), the American Hotel and Lodging Motel

Association (AH&LA), the American Dietetics Association (ADA), and others like them regularly provide their membership with legislative updates.

- Problems can arise when those who do not understand the hospitality industry propose legislation that will result in costs or infringement upon individual rights that far exceed the societal value of implementing the proposed regulation.

- It is critical that you take an active role in shaping the regulations that affect your industry.

Key Terms & Concepts Review: Quiz #1

This key terms and concepts quiz is designed to help you learn and better understand important chapter concepts and improve your Human Resources-related vocabulary.

Match the key terms with their correct definitions.

1. Employment law _____   a. A court-ordered method of debt collection in which a portion of a worker's income is paid directly to one or more of that worker's creditors.

2. Unemployment compensation _____   b. Commercial trading or the transportation of persons or property between or among states.

3. Workers' compensation _____   c. The specific section of the Civil Rights Act of 1964 that outlaws discrimination in employment in any business on the basis of race, color, religion, sex, or national origin.

4. Garnish(ment) _____   d. The body of laws, administrative rulings, and precedents that addresses the legal rights of workers and their employers.

5. Labor union _____   e. A benefit paid to an employee who suffers a work-related injury or illness.

6. Interstate commerce _____   f. The entity within the federal government assigned to enforcing the provisions of Title VII of the Civil Rights Act of 1964.

7. Title VII _____   g. An organization that acts on behalf of its members to negotiate with management about the wages, hours, and other terms and conditions of the membership's employment.

8. EEOC _____   h. A benefit paid to an employee who involuntarily loses his or her employment without just cause.

Key Terms & Concepts Review: Quiz #2

This key terms and concepts quiz is designed to help you learn and better understand important chapter concepts and improve your Human Resources-related vocabulary.

Match the key terms with their correct definitions.

1. Sexual Harassment _____   a.   The claim that, in the same situation, one employee was treated differently than other employees.

2. Affirmative action _____   b.   The business entity that has sold or granted a franchise.

3. BFOQ _____   c.   The claim that an employer's action, though not intentionally discriminatory, still results in unlawful discrimination.

4. Disparate treatment _____   d.   Unwelcome sexual advances, requests for sexual favors, and other verbal or physical conduct of a sexual nature.

5. Disparate (adverse) impact _____   e.   A specific job requirement for a particular position that is reasonably necessary to the normal operation of a business, and thus allowing discrimination against a protected class.

6. Franchisor _____   f.   Any modification or adjustment to a job or the work environment that will enable a qualified applicant or employee with a disability to participate in the application process or to perform the job's essential functions.

7. Reasonable accommodation _____   g.   A federally mandated requirement that employers who meet certain criteria must actively seek to fairly employ recognized classes of workers.

8. Expatriate manager _____   h.   The individual with the final on-site decision-making authority at an individual hospitality operation.

9. Unit manager _____   i.   A citizen of one country who is a working manager in another country.

Practice Quiz

To help you test your mastery of the chapter's content, choose the letter of the best answer to each of the questions listed below.

1. The wages of an employee may be garnished due to:
   A. Worker's compensation
   B. The Consolidated Omnibus Budget Reconciliation Act (COBRA)
   C. Legally owed debt
   D. Disparate treatment
Page 32

2. Which question CAN legally be asked on a job application or in a job interview?
   A. Have you ever been treated for drug addiction or alcoholism?
   B. Are you pregnant?
   C. What is your date of birth?
   D. Are you taking any prescription drugs?
Pages 39, 46

3. Which piece of legislation served to outlaw discrimination in employment in any business on the basis of race, color, religion, sex, or national origin:
   A. The Wagner Act
   B. The Fair Labor Standards Act
   C. The Clayton Act
   D. The Civil Rights Act
Page 33

4. The *best* way to stay informed about changes to HR-related government legislation is by:
   A. Watching for reports on the nightly news
   B. Listening to co-workers
   C. Waiting for updates from the GM
   D. Reading hospitality journals and publications
Page 56

5. Provision of a safe working environment and submission to periodic inspections is most likely required by the following?
   A. A Corporation
   B. The Government
   C. The Unit Manager
   D. An Expatriate Manager
Page 31

6. According to the Age Discrimination in Employment Act it is illegal to ask for an employee's date of birth unless:
    A. The ADEA does not specifically prohibit an employers for asking for an employee's date of birth
    B. That person appears to be 65 or older
    C. That person appears to be 16 or younger
    D. That person voluntarily offers their date of birth
Page 39

7. The Family and Medical Leave Act would allow unpaid leave for:
    A. An individual whose fiancée has a serious illness
    B. An individual whose mother has a serious illness
    C. An individual who has been the victim of domestic violence
    D. A parent who must attend parent-teacher conferences at their child's school
Page 47

8. Which of the following is NOT considered a "reasonable accommodation" for an employee with a disability:
    A. Extra unpaid leave when it does not present a hardship to the business
    B. Restructuring a job to shift a minor responsibility for a task from a disabled to a non-disabled employee
    C. Eliminating a primary job responsibility
    D. Adjusted arrival or departure times
Page 44

9. The amount of paid vacation time allotted to workers around the world:
    A. Is not standard and varies widely
    B. Is always a mandated 2 weeks
    C. Is never less than 10 days
    D. Is never more than 3 weeks
Page 53

10. Which of the following is an example of a good source for information about local level changes in municipal regulations:
    A. Franchisor updates
    B. Local police
    C. The NRA or AH&LA
    D. Federal Agencies
Page 57

For Your Consideration

The Family and Medical Leave Act (FMLA) was quite controversial when it was originally enacted in 1993. It was one of the first major bills signed by newly elected President Bill Clinton. It had previously been vetoed by the president (H.W. Bush) as an undue burden on business. The history of the FMLA provides HR managers with a recent and continuing example of how employment laws in the United States are proposed, debated in the public arena, and, in many cases, enacted. As you learned in this chapter, to be eligible for FMLA benefits, an employee must:

- Work for a covered employer
- Have worked for the employer for a total of 12 months
- Have worked at least 1,250 hours over the previous 12 months
- Work at a location where at least 50 employees are employed by the employer within 75 miles.

Assume that a popular national politician had made a proposal to expand the act by offering FMLA benefits to employees immediately upon hiring (rather than after 12 months of employment). Would you support such an expansion? What specific actions would you take in seeking to influence the vote on this proposed change in FMLA benefits? Most importantly, what factors would influence your decision?

Chapter 3
Human Resources Management: Policies and Procedures

Learning Objectives Review

At the conclusion of this chapter, you will be able to:

1. Recognize and describe the difference between the HR policies and HR procedures utilized by employers.

2. Identify the steps managers use to develop HR management policies and procedures.

3. Understand the importance of seeking legal counsel and/or review prior to implementing HR policies and procedures.

4. Recognize and appreciate the role advanced technology is currently playing, and will continue to play, in the process of HR-related policy and procedure development.

5. Recognize the most significant reasons why HR managers must develop, implement, and maintain effective HR recordkeeping systems.

Study Notes

The following is composed of important points from each chapter. Key terms are located in boxes for easy recognition.

1. HR Policy and Procedures Activities
      a. Policy and Procedure Development
      b. Areas of Policy and Procedure Development

a. Policy and Procedures Development

- Note that there is an important relationship between what your business will do (its HR policies) and exactly how you will do it (its HR procedures).

> **HR policy(ies)**: A course of action selected from alternatives and designed to guide future decision making.

- In some cases, the line between what businesses do and how they do it can be a fine one. However, it is important to remember that, to be effective, HR policies must be supported by procedures that, when followed, ensure the fair and consistent application of the policy.

b. Areas of Policy and Procedure Development

- As experienced managers know, it is not possible to identify all of the subjects within every hospitality operation that require written policies and procedures. Clearly, the policy and procedures needs of a large, multinational hospitality organization will be very different from the needs of a small, independently owned sandwich shop.

- The recruitment and selection of employees is probably the area that most hospitality managers think of first when they consider the work of the HR department or the HR manager.

> **Garde-manger**: Pantry chef. Responsible for cold food production, including salads, salad dressings, cold appetizers, charcuterie items, terrines, and similar dishes.

> **Saucier**: Sauté station chef. Responsible for all sautéed items, including most sauces.

- In non-hotel operations, but in much the same manner as the previous example, before employees can be recruited, their skill requirements must be established.

- It is important to recall that the specific requirements of current labor law mandate that managers thoroughly understand the specific skills required for the jobs they advertise. Identifying and documenting those specific skill sets effectively helps limit the potential legal liability that could be incurred if particular groups of employees are ultimately excluded from the search process.

- After the most critical characteristics related to a job's successful candidates have been carefully identified (see Chapter 6, "Position Analysis" discussion), the two most important staffing-related tasks facing the HR manager are:
  1. Ensuring an adequate pool of qualified applicants to maximize the operation's chances to hire an outstanding candidate
  2. Providing enough job information to discourage unqualified job applicants to help prevent the organization from wasting time and resources in the interviewing process

- After new employees are selected, orienting these new employees to the organization becomes an important HR function. Even experienced employees who need little or virtually no skill training will still need to learn much about their new employer.

- The best of HR managers, whether serving the dual role of unit manager or heading a large HR department, know that planning for the future staffing needs of their organization is an ongoing process.

- Regardless of the individual within the organization who will actually do the training, it remains the HR manager's role to ensure that the training is provided and to develop the legally defensible policies and procedures required to do so.

- One helpful way to consider the role of HR managers in policy and procedure development related to employee motivation is to consider two factors that are commonly agreed to affect worker motivation. These are an employee's:

  1. Ability to do a job
  2. Willingness to do a job

- Policies and procedures related to the maintenance of employees include those that help encourage quality workers to stay with the organization. Major areas of concern include worker health and safety, as well as the development and implementation of Employee Assistance Programs *(EAPs)*.

- **Employee Assistance Program:** The term used to describe a variety of employer-initiated efforts to assist employees in the areas of family concerns, legal issues, financial matters, and health maintenance.

---

2. Steps in HR Policy and Procedure Development

- To help minimize the negative consequences that can be associated with improperly developing or applying HR policies, experienced managers should establish a basic policy and procedure development process.

Six-Step Policy and Procedure Development Process

STEP	RATIONALE
1. Identify the HR issue to be addressed.	1. Policies and procedures typically are developed to address an important issue, establish a standard, or solve an identifiable problem.
2. Consider on-site factors affecting implementation.	Internal factors directly affecting the development of the policy or procedures are considered next. Examples include items such as the existence of a union contract, the objectives management seeks to achieve, and the time frame required for implementation.

3. Consider off-site factors affecting implementation.	Off-site factors that may need to be considered in the policy and procedure development process include overriding chain or franchise policies, local labor-related legislation, and competitor policies.
4. Draft policy and procedures and submit for (legal) review.	After a policy and the procedures required to implement it have been drafted, it is always a good idea to have the draft examined by a qualified legal expert. This step is important in helping to reduce potential litigation directly related to the policy.
5. Develop related documentation and recordkeeping requirements.	After a legal review has been undertaken and completed, managers will develop the recordkeeping procedures needed to ensure the consistent application of the policy, as well as the ability to prove it has indeed been applied consistently.
6. Communicate finalized policy and procedures to affected parties.	HR policies and procedures that have not been adequately communicated to those affected are difficult or may even be impossible to enforce. The final step in policy development and implementation is the policy's clear and timely communication to all affected parties, as well as the documentation of that communication.

3. Review for Legal Compliance

- While experienced HR managers understand that the manner in which a policy is implemented can be flawed, a policy that is already flawed or illegal from the outset simply should not be implemented.

- In nearly all cases, hospitality managers such can (and often do) legally impose rules and guidelines that have a basis in social norms, such as those prohibiting visible tattoos, body piercing, or earrings for men.

- It is not uncommon for hospitality employees to challenge even well-designed dress codes on the basis of purported discrimination related to their sex, race, or religion.

- Dress requirements that reflect current social norms generally are upheld, even when they affect only one sex. For example, in a decision by the Eleventh Circuit Court of Appeals in Harper v. Blockbuster Entertainment *Corp.*, 139 F.3d 1385 (11th Cir. 1998), the court upheld an employer's policy that required only male employees to cut their long hair.

- Virtually any of the areas in which policies and procedures are developed may be the source of litigation, but managers must be most careful in the areas related to the control of employee dress, expression of opinion, and behavior away from the worksite.

4. Applying Advanced Technology to HR Policies and Procedures

- In most cases, two extremely important functions of HR and, as a result, two areas where HR-related technology can be effectively utilized include information dissemination and information storage.

Hard copy: The common term for a document that has been printed on paper.

Personal file: A record of information about a single employee's employment. Typically, this file includes information about the employee's personal status, application, performance evaluations, and disciplinary warnings. Also known as a *personnel file*.

Employee handbook: A permanent reference guide for employers and employees that contains information about a company, its goals, and its current employment policies and procedures. Also often referred to as the *employee manual*.

- It is important for managers to understand that the courts will generally allow employers wide latitude to enforce a variety of job-related policies and procedures. In most cases, however, those employers must first conclusively show that their employees were, in fact, informed about the policies and procedures.

- Documenting an employee's actual receipt of important policy and procedure information is imperative.

Information storage: The processes, equipment, and documents that make up a company's records retention effort.

- Many HR managers actually find that information storage is one of their greatest challenges.

Server: A central computer system that stores documents and information for input and retrieval.

DVD: Short for **d**igital **v**ersatile **d**isc or **d**igital **v**ideo **d**isc, the DVD is a type of optical disk technology similar to the CD-ROM. DVD-ROMs are commonly used as a medium for digital representation of movies and other multimedia presentations that combine sound with graphics.

---

5. HR Policies and Procedures Documentation and record keeping

- Regardless of the level of technology they apply to the process, all HR managers must follow specific laws and regulations that address employment-related documentation and recordkeeping issues.

- HR managers must make significant decisions regarding the employment records that must be retained and the length of time to retain them. In some cases, employment-related legislation will dictate the full or partial answers to questions of this type.

Constructive discharge: An employee-initiated termination of employment brought about by conditions that make the employee's work situation so intolerable that a reasonable person would feel compelled to quit. Also known as constructive *wrongful* discharge.

RFI: An official EEOC Request for Information. An EEOC requirement that the accused party submit all requested copies of personnel policies, the accuser's personnel files, the personnel files of other individuals, and any other information deemed relevant by the EEOC.

- Most hospitality managers would agree that it is critical for large, multiunit operators to have well-documented employee-related policies and procedures in place, despite the enormity of the task. Even for very small hospitality operators, while the effort required to address the task may be lessened, in today's litigious society, its successful completion is no less critical.

Key Terms & Concepts Review: Quiz #1

This key terms and concepts quiz is designed to help you learn and better understand important chapter concepts and improve your Human Resources-related vocabulary.

Match the key terms with their correct definitions.

1. HR policy(ies) _____

     a.   Pantry chef. Responsible for cold food production, including salads, salad dressings, cold appetizers, charcuterie items, terrines, and similar dishes.

2. HR procedures _____

     b.   Sauté station chef. Responsible for all sautéed items, including most sauces.

3. Garde-manger _____

     c.   A course of action selected from alternatives and designed to guide future decision making.

4. Patissier _____

     d.   A record of information about a single employee's employment. Typically, this file includes information about the employee's personal status, application, performance evaluations, and disciplinary warnings. Also known as a *personnel file.*

5. Saucier _____

     e.   The common term for a document that has been printed on paper.

6. Employee Assistance Program _____

     f.   The entity within the federal government assigned to enforcing the provisions of Title VII of the Civil Rights Act of 1964.

7. Hard copy _____

     g.   Pastry chef. Responsible for all baked items, including breads, pastries, and desserts.

8. Personal file _____

     h.   The term used to describe a variety of employer-initiated efforts to assist employees in the areas of family concerns, legal issues, financial matters, and health maintenance.

Key Terms & Concepts Review: Quiz #2

This key terms and concepts quiz is designed to help you learn and better understand important chapter concepts and improve your Human Resources-related vocabulary.

Match the key terms with their correct definitions.

1. Employee handbook _____

    a. The processes, equipment, and documents that make up a company's records retention effort.

2. Employee manual _____

    b. An employee-initiated termination of employment brought about by conditions that make the employee's work situation so intolerable that a reasonable person would feel compelled to quit. Also known as constructive *wrongful* discharge.

3. Information storage _____

    c. A compact disc is a device capable of storing digital information. CD-ROM (read-only memory) means that once the data has been recorded onto the CD, it can only be read or played, but not revised.

4. Server _____

    d. An official EEOC Request for Information. An EEOC requirement that the accused party submit all requested copies of personnel policies, the accuser's personnel files, the personnel files of other individuals, and any other information deemed relevant by the EEOC.

5. CD _____

    e. Short for digital versatile disc or digital video disc, the DVD is a type of optical disk technology similar to the CD-ROM. DVD-ROMs are commonly used as a medium for digital representation of movies and other multimedia presentations that combine sound with graphics.

6. DVD _____

    f. A central computer system that stores documents and information for input and retrieval.

7. Constructive discharge _____

    g. Same as *employee handbook*.

8. RFI _____

    h. A permanent reference guide for employers and employees that contains information about a company, its goals, and its current employment policies and procedures.

Practice Quiz

To help you test your mastery of the chapter's content, choose the letter of the best answer to each of the questions listed below.

1. Abraham Maslow's motivation theory of Needs Hierarchy states that the following is a person's most basic need which must be met first:
    A. Esteem
    B. Physiological needs
    C. Actualization
    D. Love/Belonging
Page 72

2. The ability to have multiple levels of security in a record keeping system is important because:
    A. It ensures that information is not lost
    B. It ensures that hard copies are easily attained
    C. It ensures that sensitive information is protected
    D. It ensures a dedicated server
Page 85

3. The following employee would posses the skills of preparing salads and cold appetizers:
    A. Gardener
    B. Garde-manger
    C. Patissier
    D. Saucier
Page 69

4. The following dress code policy has been successfully enforced without being considered discriminatory:
    A. All have been judged to have the potential for discrimination in some cases
    B. Prohibition of beards
    C. Prohibition of union insignia
    D. Prohibition of head coverings
Pages 78-79

5. The following is NOT an effective way to ensure that an organization's HR policies keep from violating laws:
    A. Purchase pre-written policies and procedures
    B. Ignore new policies that are listed in hospitality magazines
    C. Seek legal counsel prior to implementing HR policies and procedures
    D. Engage in a periodic legal review of the overall policy and procedures manual
Page 77

6. The following is an example of a procedure:
   A. Dress and uniform codes
   B. Employee selection criteria
   C. Constructive discharge
   D. Requiring written documentation in cases of employee termination
Page 65

7. The most effective way of documenting that all staff members have read and understood the company's employee handbook is:
   A. Have the HR manager read the handbook aloud for each new employee
   B. Supply each employee with a new, updated copy of the handbook each year
   C. Have each employee sign a document stating they have read and understood the handbook, then place a copy in the employee's personal file
   D. Have one copy of the handbook available in the GM's office so interested employees can consult it
Page 81

8. Employee Assistance Programs are intended to:
   A. Help hospitality operations avoid expensive litigation for violating governmental regulations
   B. Encourage employees make claims against employers through the EEOC
   C. Eliminate employee turn-over
   D. Assist employees in the areas of family concerns, legal issues, financial matters and health maintenance
Page 73

9. A "Request for Information" can require that a company:
   A. Research an employee's home town
   B. Allow an employee access to the files of another employee
   C. A company cannot be required to reveal information to anyone
   D. Submit personnel files and other relevant information to the EEOC
Page 89

10. The following is agreed to have the largest effect on worker motivation:
    A. Intrapreneurship
    B. Legal recruiting practices
    C. Workers' ability and willingness to do a job
    D. Size of the HR department
Page 71

For Your Consideration

More than a third of people ages 18-25 have tattoos, and 40% of people 26-40 have them, says a recently conducted Pew Research Center study. Thanks to cable TV shows such as Miami Ink, L.A. Ink, and London Ink, the acceptance of tattoos is growing. Most businesses, however, still prohibit visible tattoos on employees. Assume you were asked to be a part of a joint employee-management committee convened to review your firm's dress code. Currently, visible tattoos are not permitted.

Would you support an employee initiated suggestion that visible tattoos be permitted? What factors would likely influence your own support of a policy change that would allow this type of visible body art?

Chapter 4
Employee Recruitment and Selection

Learning Objectives Review

At the conclusion of this chapter, you will be able to:

1. Identify the factors that HR managers must consider prior to planning and initiating their organization's employee recruitment efforts.

2. Differentiate between the actions HR managers take when electing to conduct internal, external, or outsourced searches for qualified employees.

3. List and explain the importance of applications, interviews, testing, background checks, and references—the five major activities that HR managers undertake when screening employees for possible selection.

4. Understand and explain the potential legal liability related to negligent hiring.

5. Describe the legal differences between a conditional job offer and a final job offer.

Study Notes

The following is composed of important points from each chapter. Key terms are located in boxes for easy recognition.

1. Factors Affecting Recruiting Efforts

-   One characteristic that has historically distinguished the hospitality industry from others is the ability of a single, innovative entrepreneur to make a remarkable impact.
-   Employee recruitment and selection efforts are critical to the long-term success of every hospitality business and to all of the hospitality managers who direct their operation's recruitment and selection process.
-   In the hospitality industry, successful managers focus on two very different, but related tasks. These are:
    1. Securing and keeping an adequate customer base
    2. Securing and keeping an adequate number of qualified employees to serve the customer base

> **Recruiting**: The process of identifying candidates for current or future position vacancies.

> **Selection**: The process of choosing an individual for a current or future position vacancy.

- In most cases, hospitality managers will find that the hourly employees they hire must undergo specific skills training before they become fully productive workers.

- Hospitality managers should understand and appreciate other, more important nonskill issues, when considering the factors that directly affect their employee recruitment efforts.

- In the hospitality industry, managers must recognize existing legal, economic, industry, organizational, and positions constraints, discussed as follows:

  - *Legal constraints*. As you learned in Chapter 2, local, state, and federal laws significantly affect a hospitality manager's efforts in recruiting employees. An employer can no longer seek out preferred individuals based on non-job-related factors such as age, gender, or physical attractiveness. Those that do so may be confronted with significant legal problems. For example, in the hospitality industry, it is simply inappropriate to view positions as being best suited for males or females. Historically, the hospitality and tourism industries have provided tremendous opportunities for employees of all backgrounds, and they will continue to do so, not only because it is the legal thing to do, but because it is the right thing to do.

  - *Economic constraints*. Economic constraints affect both the organization that is recruiting employees and the employees themselves. In many cases, the wages and salaries that can be paid to workers and managers are directly determined by the profitability of the operation for which they will work. If, for example, the operation must maintain a targeted, predetermined labor budget, or achieve its labor cost percentage goal, it will likely be restricted in the amount of money it can offer new employees. All organizations face such economic restraints, and thus this challenge is simply one more that can be addressed and overcome by professional hospitality managers.

  - *Industry constraints*. Some individuals truly do not understand the hospitality industry well. As a result, they view it as one in which opportunities for personal advancement are few, and the remuneration offered for working is low. In fact, the hospitality industry offers significant personal and financial rewards for workers with a variety of backgrounds, from those with limited formal education to those with advanced professional degrees. It is unlikely that any single HR manager will change industry perceptions, but it is important to understand that recruitments efforts should, when necessary, directly address potential candidate biases.

- *Organizational constraints.* Just as some applicants will have a general reaction to jobs advertised within the hospitality industry, others may react to the specific organization for which the job is advertised. For example, foodservice managers operating school foodservice units may find that their jobs are perceived very positively because of an assessment by applicants that these jobs will have traditional hours, may come with above-average benefits, and allow the worker to be off-work in the summer. Alternatively, managers operating high-energy nightclubs in larger cities will likely find that their best potential applicants are drawn to the excitement of their operations, although most of their jobs will require them to work during nontraditional (extremely late-night) hours.

- *Position constraints.* In the hospitality industry, some jobs are perceived as glamorous, while others are not. If the position a manager seeks to fill is unattractive to most workers, recruiting a large and qualified pool of applicants will likely be challenging. In recent years, more hospitality managers have been complaining about the difficulty of finding suitably qualified individuals for manual labor positions such as dishwashers, janitors, landscaping and grounds care, room attendants, and others. In job markets where the unemployment rate is low, and where a wide range of opportunity creates competition, a worker shortage may exist. In cases such as these, qualified applicants may be difficult to find, so managers must work diligently and creatively to locate potential applicants who can bring great value to their organizations.

Unemployment rate: A government statistic that measures the percentage of workers who are not employed, but who are seeking work.

---

2. The Search for Qualified Employees

    a. Internal Search
    b. External Search
    c. Outsourced Search

- Hospitality managers at all levels and in all sizes of organizations will continually find that they must actively recruit employees. From company presidents to the lowest-skilled *entry-level* employee, candidate recruitment will usually be an ongoing activity.

Entry-level: The position in which an individual starts his or her career with a hospitality organization.

a. Internal Search

Internal search: A promotion-from-within approach that is utilized when seeking qualified job applicants

Employee referral: A recommendation about a potential applicant that is provided by a current employee.

- Employee referral systems tend to work well because employees rarely recommend someone unless they feel that person can do a good job and will fit well into the organization

Nepotism: Favoritism in employment based on kinship.

b. External Search

External search: An approach to seeking job applicants that focuses primarily on those candidates who are not currently employed by the organization.

- When organizations seek candidates externally, they rely on a variety of strategies, including advertisements, public and private employment assistance agencies, educational institutions, and unsolicited applications.

Blind ad: A job advertisement that does not identify the advertising organization. Also known as a *blind-box ad*.

c. Outsourced Search

- **Outsourced search**: A search for job candidates that is performed by a professional company specializing in employee searches.

- **Executive search**: A private employment agency that specializes in identifying candidates for management positions. Also known as head hunter firms.

- It is important to understand that, in most cases, HR managers do not choose from among internal, external, and outsourcing as their sole method of recruiting. Rather, the best managers select the approach appropriate for the vacancy they seek to fill. In some cases, this will result in using more than one of the strategies, or even all three of them when seeking to fill a specific position.

3. Factors Affecting Selections Efforts

a. Application
b. Interviews
c. Testing
d. Background Checks
e. References

a. Application

- If, as a manager, you are responsible for developing your own application, it is a good idea to have the document reviewed by a legal specialist prior to using it.
- It is also important that each employment candidate for a given position be required to fill out an identical application, and that an application be on file for each candidate who is ultimately selected for the position. In addition, it is also a good practice for the application to clearly state the at-will nature of the employment relationship.

- **At-will (employment)**: An employment relationship in which either party can, at any time, terminate the relationship with no liability.

---

b. Interviews

- It is important for HR managers to understand that the types of questions that can be asked in the interview are highly restricted. This is because job interviews, if improperly performed, can subject managers to significant legal liability.
- The EEOC suggests that an employer consider the following three issues when deciding whether to include a particular question on an employment application or to ask it in a job interview:
  1. Does this question tend to screen out minorities or females?
  2. Is the answer needed in order to judge this individual's competence for performance of the job?
  3. Are there alternative, nondiscriminatory ways, to judge the person's qualifications?

c. Testing

- In the hospitality industry, pre-employment testing will generally fall into one of the following categories:

    1. Skills tests
    2. Psychological tests
    3. Drug screening tests

- If you elect to implement either a pre-employment or post-employment drug-testing program, it is best to first seek advice from an attorney who specializes in labor employment law in your state.

d. Background Checks

- It has been estimated that as many as 35 percent of all résumés and employment applications include some level of falsification. Because this is true, employers are spending more time and financial resources to validate information supplied by a potential employee.

- As a general rule, criminal conviction records should be checked when there is a possibility that the person could create significant safety or security risks for coworkers, guests, or clients. Examples include employees who will (1) have close contact with minors, the elderly, the disabled, or patients; (2) have access to weapons, drugs, chemicals, or other potentially dangerous materials; (3) work in, or deliver goods to, customers' homes; and (4) handle money or other valuables, or have access to financial information or employee personal information.

- The use of credit reports should be limited to situations where there is a legitimate business justification, such as for jobs that entail monetary responsibilities, the use of financial discretion, or similar security risks.

- MVRs should be checked for any employee who will drive a company vehicle or a personal vehicle on the employer's business.

- Academic information (such as schools attended, degrees awarded, and transcripts) should be verified when a specified level or type of education is necessary for a particular job.

e. References

- Personal references have become a much greater recruiting tool than references from past employers.

- As an employer, you and your own organization must be extremely cautious in both giving and receiving reference information. Employers are usually protected if they give a truthful reference, but that does not mean you will be free from the time and expense of defending a defamation case brought by an ex-employee.

> **Defamation**: False statements that cause someone to be held in contempt, lowered in the estimation of the community, or to lose employment status or earnings, or otherwise suffer a damaged reputation.

- To minimize your own risk of a lawsuit, you should never reply to a request for information about one of your ex-employees without a copy of that employee's signed release authorizing the reference check.

4. Negligent Hiring

> **Negligent hiring**: Failure on the part of an employer to exercise reasonable care in the selection of employees.

> **Negligent retention**: Retaining an employee after the employer became aware of an employee's unsuitability for a job, thereby failing to act on that knowledge.

- Negligent hiring liability is usually found where an employee who caused injury or harm to another had a reputation or record that showed his or her propensity to do so, and this record would have been easily discoverable by that employer, had reasonable care (in this case, a diligent search) been shown.

- All that is normally required to show that reasonable care was used in the hiring process is to thoroughly verify all pertinent information about each candidate prior to making a job offer.

5. Job Offers

> **Employment agreement**: The terms of the employment relationship between an employer and employee that specify the rights and obligations of each party to the agreement.

- To avoid difficulties, all employees should have signed offer letters in their personnel files. Components of a sound offer letter include:
    1. Position being offered
    2. Compensation included

3. Benefits included (if any)
4. Evaluation period and compensation review schedule
5. Start date
6. Location of employment
7. Special conditions of the offer (i.e., the at-will relationship)
8. Reference to the employment manual (see Chapter 3) as an additional source of information regarding employer policies that govern the workplace
9. Signature lines for both employer and employee
10. Date of signature lines

- An offer letter may be either conditional or final.

- When putting forward a conditional offer letter, the employer tentatively, or conditionally, offers the job, but the offer is subject to the conditions that must be met by the applicant before the job offer is finalized.

- A final offer letter contains no conditions that must be met before acceptance. An enforceable employment contract is in effect at such time as the final offer letter is legally accepted by the job applicant.

Key Terms & Concepts Review: Quiz #1

This key terms and concepts quiz is designed to help you learn and better understand important chapter concepts and improve your Human Resources-related vocabulary.

Match the key terms with their correct definitions.

1. Recruiting _____

2. Selection _____

3. Unemployment rate _____

4. Internal search _____

5. Promote-from-within _____

6. Employee referral _____

7. Nepotism _____

8. External search _____

9. Blind ad

a. A promotion-from-within approach that is utilized when seeking qualified job applicants.

b. An approach to seeking job applicants that focuses primarily on those candidates who are not currently employed by the organization.

c. A recommendation about a potential applicant that is provided by a current employee.

d. The process of identifying candidates for current or future position vacancies.

e. A job advertisement that does not identify the advertising organization. Also known as a *blind-box ad*.

f. A government statistic that measures the percentage of workers who are not employed, but who are seeking work.

g. An organizational philosophy that, whenever practical, an organization will fill its higher-level job vacancies with its current lower-level employees.

h. The process of choosing an individual for a current or future position vacancy.

i Favoritism in employment based on kinship.

Key Terms & Concepts Review: Quiz #2

This key terms and concepts quiz is designed to help you learn and better understand important chapter concepts and improve your Human Resources-related vocabulary.

Match the key terms with their correct definitions.

1. Unemployment benefits _____

    a. An employment relationship in which either party can, at any time, terminate the relationship with no liability.

2. Outsourced search _____

    b. Failure on the part of an employer to exercise reasonable care in the selection of employees.

3. Executive search _____

    c. Retaining an employee after the employer became aware of an employee's unsuitability for a job, thereby failing to act on that knowledge.

4. At-will (employment) _____

    d. A search for job candidates that is performed by a professional company specializing in employee searches.

5. Defamation _____

    e. Monetary and nonmonetary resources given to those who are jobless but who are actively seeking work. presentations that combine sound with graphics.

6. Negligent hiring _____

    f. The terms of the employment relationship between an employer and employee that specify the rights and obligations of each party to the agreement.

7. Negligent retention _____

    g. A proposal by an employer to a prospective employee that specifies the terms of employment. A legally valid acceptance of the offer will create a binding employment contract.

8. Employment agreement _____

    h. False statements that cause someone to be held in contempt, lowered in the estimation of the community, or to lose employment status or earnings, or otherwise suffer a damaged reputation.

9. Offer letter

    i. A private employment agency that specializes in identifying candidates for management positions. Also known as head hunter firms.

Practice Quiz

To help you test your mastery of the chapter's content, choose the letter of the best answer to each of the questions listed below.

1. Inbreeding and lack of new ideas can at times be a by-product of this type of recruitment:
   A. Internal recruitment
   B. External recruitment
   C. Unsolicited applications
   D. Outsourced search
Page 106

2. Employers, at the time of hire, are required by law to obtain valid identification documents from:
   A. All employees
   B. Only those employees who have immigrated to the country in the last 5 years
   C. Only those employees who still have family members living over-seas
   D. Only those employees who appear to be foreign-born
Page 102

3. This kind of employee search is most likely to build employee morale:
   A. Blind Ads
   B. Employee Referral
   C. Outsourced Search
   D. External Search
Page 106

4. At the time that an employee submits their Employment Eligibility Verification Form (I-9), it is the employer's responsibility to do all of the following EXCEPT:
   A. Legally verify the authenticity of the identification documents
   B. Retain copies of the identification documents
   C. Assure that the documents are submitted within 72 hours of the time of hire
   D. Confirm that the identification documents *appear* valid and real
Page 126

5. During the hiring of entry-level staff, often a candidate's _____ can be much more important than their _____.
   A. Prior experience; Work ethic
   B. Background; Friendliness
   C. Attitude; Prior experience
   D. Internal recruiting; External recruiting
Page 101

6. Perceptions of the hospitality industry can lead potential job candidates to believe hospitality jobs offer little hope for promotion and low compensation rates. Efforts to correct this inaccurate image should focus on the fact that jobs in the hospitality industry:
    A. Offer good job stability
    B. Allow one to utilize personal creativity
    C. Feature a team environment
    D. All of the above

Page 104

7. The following is NOT considered a major selection activity when an employer is selecting an applicant:
    A. Pre-employment testing
    B. Outsourced searching
    C. References
    D. Interviews

Page 113

8. If an organization wishes to replace a current employee with a new one, without letting the employee know that a replacement search is underway, they would most likely:
    A. Promote from within
    B. Outsource the search
    C. Accept an employee referral
    D. Place a blind ad

Page 108

9. A potential job-seeker is dissuaded from looking for employment within a hospitality operation because of her perception that work in the field of hospitality offers little opportunity for personal advancement. Efforts by a Human Resources Manager to change that perception and create a more positive view of hospitality jobs in general would mean working against a(n) _____.
    A. Position Constraint
    B. Economic Constraint
    C. Industry Constraint
    D. Organizational Constraint

Page 103

10. A conditional offer letter states that a position will be offered to a prospective employee only after:
    A. The employee has satisfactorily completed 10-14 days of work
    B. An application is submitted
    C. The employee satisfactorily fulfills specific requirements, such as passing a drug test or background check
    D. The employee does nothing

Page 128

For Your Consideration

Now that you have finished reading this chapter, read the following mini-case:

"There is something you should know" said Jeremiah Delry, "I have AIDS."

Jeremiah was talking to JeAnna Tennety, the HR manager of the City Plaza Hotel.

JeAnna was interviewing Jeremiah for a banquet waiter's position because of his years of experience as a waiter, his friendly personality and his willingness to work the busy hours when JeAnna needed additional staff.

Jeremiah relayed to JeAnna that he had left his previous position because there had been open grumbling and rampant rumors from some of the other employees regarding his sexual orientation, and because of his illness, the appropriateness of his working in a restaurant.

Jeremiah had taken it upon himself to address JeAnna about it because he wanted her to hear it from him first, and he wanted to ask, if he were hired, if there were anything he could do to help JeAnna and the hotel avoid a similar situation.

In this instance, what do you believe are JeAnna's hiring responsibilities relative to:

- The hotel?
- Tom?
- Her other employees?

Chapter 5
First Impressions and an Ethical Foundation

Learning Objectives Review

At the conclusion of this chapter, you will be able to:

1. Review the basic concerns of new employees as they begin work in a hospitality organization.

2. Explain important procedures that should be used as employee orientation programs and procedures are developed and implemented.

3. Note the importance of employee handbooks, and list typical policy and procedure topics that might be included in them.

4. Identify basic concerns that should be addressed as employee mentoring programs are planned and implemented.

5. Discuss the role of ethics in the management of human resources.

Study Notes

The following is composed of important points from each chapter. Key terms are located in boxes for easy recognition.

1. New Employee Adaptation Process

a. Employee Adaptation Concerns
b. Steps in the Adaptation Process

a. Employee Adaptation Concerns

* Managers have an important responsibility to help their new employees learn about and become comfortable working in the hospitality operation. Whether it is planned or just happens, all newly employed staff go through an adaptation process as they learn about the values of the organization and what it's like to work for it.

> **Adaptation (to the organization):** The process by which new employees learn the values of and what it's like to work for a hospitality organization during initial on-job experiences.

- For employees to work effectively, they must know what to do, and they must perform job tasks properly.
- The cleanliness of work stations, conversations of employees between themselves and with guests, and behaviors of employees that represent their work attitudes will be observed by and will influence the attitudes and behaviors of new staff members.

b. Steps in the adaptation process

- **Step 1:** When new employees are selected, they have basic perceptions and attitudes about the work and the organization. These are probably based on factors including (a) information learned during the employment interview; (b) advertising messages (if, for example, the new employee has experienced the company's advertising messages); (c) previous experience, if any, as a guest in the operation; and (d) feedback about the property from others in the community, including present or past employees.

- **Step 2:** Early on-job experiences including orientation and training may reinforce initial perceptions (Step 1), or they may prove them to be less than accurate. Some apprehension is typical, however, if there is a significant difference between what new employees perceived (Step 1) and what they actually experience (Step 2). New staff members must either make significant changes in perceptions and expectations or, perhaps more frequently, new employees are likely to become discontented and become additional turnover statistics. This is especially so when the new employee desires to work for an organization in a position that meets initial expectations (Step 1), and/or when the staff member has other employment opportunities, which often occurs when there are high unemployment rates.

- **Step 3:** Employees who begin to recognize and accept the culture of the organization and who want to become cooperating members of work teams will likely be accepted by their peers. They then want to become contributing members of the organization.

- **Step 4:** At this point, perhaps the most difficult challenge has been accomplished. The new staff member has a positive attitude about the organization and is willing to learn about and contribute to it. The initial orientation and training activities enable new employees to perform work meeting quality and quantity standards. Successful performance reinforces the employees' attitude about the organization, and they begin to experience and relate to cultural norms encouraging retention rather than turnover.

- In large organizations, human resource managers and their line department counterparts must work closely together to best assure that the work environment is favorable to staff members. In smaller organizations without human resources specialists, managers have the increased responsibility to plan, implement, and maintain work environments that encourage employee retention.

2. Orientation Programs and Procedures

    a. Goals of Orientation Programs
    b. Use an Orientation Checklist
    c. Departmental Induction Procedures
    d. Orientation Follow-up

- Orientation is the process of providing basic information about the hospitality organization that must be known by all staff members in every department. Implemented effectively, orientation efforts provide initial on-job experiences that help new staff members learn about the organization and its purposes, become comfortable with the work environment, and learn where they fit into it.

Orientation: The process of providing basic information about the hospitality organization that must be known by all staff members in every department.

---

a. Goals of the orientation process

- Provides an overview of the organization. Many newly employed staff members want to know about their employer's history, size (e.g., number of locations and staff members), and the products and services it provides. They should learn about the results their new organization is attempting to achieve. Trainees may want to know how their organization adds value for its guests, to themselves, and to the organization's owners. A mission statement explains what the organization wants to accomplish and how it intends to do so. The mission statement should also serve as a guide for decision making and be used every day (and not just as an introductory page in an employee handbook or for a slogan on the managers' business cards).
- Indicates the new staff member's role. If you were a new staff member, would you like to see an organization chart showing all positions including yours and the reporting relationships between them? Would you like to learn where you fit in

and about promotion tracks if you perform well? You probably would, and new staff members do as well.

- Explains policies, rules, and other information. Staff want to know general guidelines, including days and hours of work, uniform requirements, break times, auto parking, and other similar information to help them feel more comfortable.
- Outlines specific expectations. Topics including responsibilities of the employer to the staff and of the staff to the employer should be addressed.
- Provides details about employee benefits. Staff members want information about nonsalary/nonwage compensation and the requirements to receive these benefits.
- Motivates new staff members. The enthusiasm and excitement exhibited by those providing orientation experiences are important. Orientation helps establish a solid foundation for the relationship between the organization, its managers and supervisors, and the new staff members.

Mission statement: A strategic statement that indicates (provides an overview of) what the hospitality organization wants to accomplish and how it intends to do so.

---

b. Use an orientation check list

- It is important to assemble all needed materials required before the orientation session begins. Some hospitality operations include these in an orientation kit.

Orientation kit: A package of written materials given to new employees to supplement the oral information provided during the orientation session.

---

c. Departmental Induction Procedures

- *Induction* relates to the process of providing new employees with basic information that everyone in their department must know that is unique to their department.

Induction: The process of providing new employees with basic information that everyone in their department must know that is unique to their department.

- An unplanned induction program can quickly destroy the benefits gained from an effective orientation program.

d. Orientation Follow-up

- Orientation follow-up activities are also important. It is not sufficient to say, "If you have any questions, just ask someone," or "Just assume you're doing okay unless someone tells you differently." New staff members should understand they will be participating in a well-organized training program designed to help them perform job tasks that meet standards.

- Employees will, one way or another, learn about the organization, their position, and their employer's expectations. It is better for them to acquire this information through a formal, planned, organized, and hospitable orientation effort than to pick it up in casual conversations with and by watching peers on the job.

3. Employee Handbooks

a. Employee Handbooks are Necessary
b. Important Policies and Procedures Are Identified

a. Employee Handbooks

- Employee handbooks tell new and all other staff members about the organization. They detail all policies and procedures to which the employer and employees agree, and they can be referenced by courts seeking to define terms of the employment agreement if disputes arise.

- Typically, employee handbooks should indicate that the hospitality operation has the right to modify, alter, or eliminate any or all contents at any time. Further, it is important to indicate within the manual that it is not a contract. The organization's attorney should be consulted as the employee handbook is developed and, most certainly, before it is circulated.

b. Important Policies and procedures are identified

- Managers can use a questioning approach to help assess what topics could be useful. Do new or longer-tenured staff members have questions about issues related to the topic? Is there an inconsistent understanding about how, if at all, an issue is managed from the perspectives of subordinate staff? These and related questions, when answered affirmatively, may determine the need for new or revised policies and procedures.

4. Mentoring Programs

    a. Background
    b. Implementing a Formal Mentoring Program

> **Mentoring**: A formal or informal relationship in which an experienced staff member provides advice and counsel to a less-experienced staff member.

a. Background

- Advantages can also accrue to mentors:

  - *Enhanced self-esteem.* A mentor will likely feel good about the   opportunity to provide advice and to make a difference.
  - *Increased knowledge.* Mentors learn as they interact with mentorees.
  - *Seen as good citizens.* Mentors may receive special consideration as their own careers are evaluated.
  - *Helps to train successors.* Sometimes mentors cannot be promoted until someone is available to assume their position, and this can be the mentoree.

- An effective mentor can serve several roles in interactions with mentorees:

  - *Trainer.* Mentors who are queried about specific on-job performance issues can provide applicable assistance and serve as an informal trainer.
  - *Coach.* Mentors can provide positive reinforcement about desired performance, and they may advise against actions that may lead to on-job difficulties, just as a supervisor does when coaching a staff member.
  - *Counselor.* Counselors do not make decisions for another person but, rather, discuss the pro and cons of a situation. They ask open-ended questions to learn what the other person is thinking and, in the process, allow the other person to more clearly think things through. A counselor provides benchmark information that can help one to evaluate personal perspectives.
  - *Guide.* Just as a guide safely leads someone who is unfamiliar with a geographic area to a destination, so can a mentor help a mentoree to move on to interim locations on the way to a longer-term destination (career).
  - *Role model.* The old saying, "Actions speak louder than words," suggests that mentorees can learn much from their mentors just by observing them as they interact with others in the organization.
  - *Advocate.* A mentor in a senior position can emphasize the strengths and abilities of a mentoree to those at higher organizational levels.

> **Career ladder**: A progression of increasingly more responsible positions within an organization or an industry.

5. Human Resources and Ethical Concerns

     a. What are Ethics?
     b. Codes of Ethics
     c. Corporate (Social) Responsibility

a.   What are Ethic's

- The concept of ethics relates to a set of rules or principles that define what is right and what is wrong. Unfortunately, these definitions can vary considerably based on the individual making the determination.

Ethics: A set of rules or principles that define what is right and what is wrong as decisions are made that affect others.

Business ethics: Refers to the practice of ethical judgment by managers as they make decisions affecting the organization.

Behavior, unethical: Actions not in concert with generally accepted social concerns relating to the impact of decisions on others.

- Some writers have offered ethical principles for hospitality managers that should be followed when decisions are made. These include:

  - *Honesty*. Don't mislead or deceive others.
  - *Integrity*. Do what is right.
  - *Trustworthiness*. Supply correct information, and correct any information that is not factual.
  - *Loyalty*. Avoid conflicts of interest, and don't disclose confidential information.
  - *Fairness*. Treat individuals equally; be tolerant of diversity.
  - *Concern and respect*. Be considerate of those impacted by decision making.
  - *Commitment to excellence*. Do the best you can do.
  - *Leadership*. Lead by example.
  - *Reputation and morale*. Work to enhance the company's reputation and the morale of employees.
  - *Accountability*. Accept responsibility for decisions that are made.[1]

- Human resources managers should recognize that their behavior often speaks more loudly than the philosophy expressed in their organization's mission statement.

b. Code of Ethics

> **Code of ethics**: A statement used by a hospitality organization to outline broad concepts to guide ethical decision making.

- Hospitality organizations typically develop codes of ethics for several reasons, including:

  - To identify a foundation of acceptable behaviors.

  - To promote standards that should guide decision making.

  - To provide a benchmark that can be used to evaluate potential decisions.

  - To support the responsibility and obligations that decision makers have to constituents and to society.

- The best codes of ethics are developed specifically for the organization, and they utilize input from the staff members who will be expected to utilize the codes.

- The support of top-level leadership is of obvious importance as codes of ethics are developed. They should be reviewed by legal counsel, and formal approval from the highest levels in the organization is required.

- A code of ethics is important, and its emphasis should last forever. It is not a program that begins and ends at specified times. All staff members should be held accountable for the behavior described in the code of ethics.

c. Corporate and Social Responsibilities

> **Corporate (social) responsibility**: Relates to an organization's efforts to address its commitments to all of its constituencies, including guests, employees, other businesses including suppliers, investors, and society, and the community-at-large.

> **Stakeholders**: Groups, individuals, and organizations that are affected by an organization; also called *constituents*.

- At this point, careful readers might be thinking, "While this is true, how exactly does corporate responsibility relate to the management of hospitality human resources?" The answer to this addresses two issues:

  - Cultural consistency. Can an organization and its leaders be concerned about three constituencies (guests, employees, and investors) without being concerned about others? Doesn't the concept of business ethics noted earlier in this chapter apply beyond the organization itself? Those who shape an organization's culture in ways that attract and retain the most qualified staff members (the primary goal of human resources) will likely treat others in ways that mirror their concern for their staff members.

- Employer-of-choice concerns. Applicants are attracted to organizations within their community that have favorable reputations. In perhaps the most simple example, networks of young people at high schools and colleges provide answers to questions for their peers such as, "What's it like to work at specific restaurants, hotels, and/or other hospitality organizations within the community?" An organization's reputation is influenced by, and is known to, many persons beyond the market of current and potential employees. Consider, for example, the impact of positive publicity that arises as organizations participation in community activities and assist with (or take a lead in) addressing broad societal concerns.

Publicity: Free-of-charge information in the media that attracts attention to an organization.

- Today's society increasingly emphasizes that its organizations be good corporate citizens, and businesses do so as they:

  - Assume a responsibility toward the environment by controlling (minimizing) the pollution of air, water, and land.

  - Accept a responsibility of concern toward guests by staying clear of unethical and irresponsible business practices relating to consumers' rights, unfair pricing, and being honest with advertising messages.

Key Terms & Concepts Review: Quiz #1

This key terms and concepts quiz is designed to help you learn and better understand important chapter concepts and improve your Human Resources-related vocabulary.

Match the key terms with their correct definitions.

1. Adaptation (to the organization) _____

2. Orientation _____

3. Mission statement _____

4. Orientation kit _____

5. Induction _____

6. Mentoring _____

7. Career ladder _____

8. Cross-functional team _____

a. A strategic statement that indicates (provides an overview of) what the hospitality organization wants to accomplish and how it intends to do so.

b. The process of providing new employees with basic information that everyone in their department must know that is unique to their department.

c. A formal or informal relationship in which an experienced staff member provides advice and counsel to a less-experienced staff member.

d. A progression of increasingly more responsible positions within an organization or an industry.

e. The process by which new employees learn the values of and what it's like to work for a hospitality organization during initial on-job experiences.

f. A group of staff members comprising representatives from different departments (functional areas) that address a common concern.

g. The process of providing basic information about the hospitality organization that must be known by all staff members in every department.

h. A package of written materials given to new employees to supplement the oral information provided during orientation.

Key Terms & Concepts Review: Quiz #2

This key terms and concepts quiz is designed to help you learn and better understand important chapter concepts and improve your Human Resources-related vocabulary.

Match the key terms with their correct definitions.

1. Ethics _____

    a. Actions not in concert with generally accepted social concerns relating to the impact of decisions on others.

2. Business ethics _____

    b. A statement used by a hospitality organization to outline broad concepts to guide ethical decision making.

3. Behavior, ethical _____

    c. Groups, individuals, and organizations that are affected by an organization; also called *constituents*.

4. Behavior, unethical _____

    d. Relates to an organization's efforts to address its commitments to all of its constituencies, including guests, employees, other businesses including suppliers, investors, and society, and the community-at-large.

5. Code of ethics _____

    e. Free-of-charge information in the media that attracts attention to an organization.

6. Corporate (social) responsibility _____

    f. A set of rules or principles that define what is right and what is wrong as decisions are made that affect others.

7. Stakeholders _____

    g. Actions in concert with generally accepted social concerns relating to the impact of decisions on others.

8. Publicity _____

    h. Refers to the practice of ethical judgment by managers as they make decisions affecting the organization.

Practice Quiz

To help you test your mastery of the chapter's content, choose the letter of the best answer to each of the questions listed below.

1. If an employee who initially had a very positive perception of their job has a poor on-job experience, it is likely that this employee will:
    A. Want to give feedback about the adaptation process
    B. Have a hard time being accepted by peers
    C. Become discontented and may eventually quit
    D. Successfully complete the steps of the adaptation process
Page 137

2. A new employee is most likely to be provided the company mission statement during:
    A. The job interview
    B. The orientation program
    C. The recruitment process
    D. The induction program
Page 140

3. An organization can _____ to encourage consistent adherence to policies and regulations outlined in the employee handbook:
    A.   Inform staff members about the reasons for the policies and procedures
    B.   Eliminate employees the first time they violate a rule
    C.   Agree to "bend the rules" the first time only
    D.   Discard those regulations which are frequently violated
Page 153

4. An organization that is concerned with corporate responsibility is also likely to be concerned about (and therefore more likely to retain) quality employees. This is an example of:
    A. Cultural consistency
    B. Poor Managing
    C. Publicity
    D. Stakeholders
Page 163

5. The person most likely to benefit from a mentoring relationship is:
    A. The mentor
    B. The mentoree
    C. The organization as a whole
    D. All of the above
Page 154

6. The following is most likely to be included in an induction program:
    A. Details about employee benefits
    B. A department tour
    C. An overview of the organization
    D. Compensation policies
Page 146

7. The following is NOT considered a goal of an orientation program:
    A. Provide an overview of the organization
    B. Detail employee benefits
    C. Motivate new staff members
    D. Give department-specific job information
Page 140

8. A mentor is in a great position to assist a _____ in developing a career ladder:
    A. Long term employees
    B. Mentoree
    C. Mentor
    D. The front desk operator
Page 155

9. All of the following factors contribute to the initial perceptions and attitudes a new employee has about an organization EXCEPT:
    A. Information learned during their interview
    B. Previous experience as a guest in the operation
    C. Advertising messages
    D. Purchasing new clothes for the job
Page 137

10. In order to avoid legal problems, it is a good idea to provide which of the following to new employees:
    A. Information about sexual harassment complaint procedures
    B. Information about Americans with Disabilities Act concerns
    C. Information about responsible alcohol service
    D. All of the above
Page 141

For Your Consideration

The philosophy of ethics has been defined as the study of principles relating to right and wrong conduct. Much of the conduct that a society considers to be wrong will also be classified as a crime. Not all wrong conduct, however, is considered illegal. Some wrong conduct is legal; but unethical. Consider the segment of the hospitality industry in which you are interested in working. What are some specific activities or behaviors which could occur in that segment that, while legal, you would consider to be unethical?

Chapter 6
Planning Training Programs

Learning Objectives Review

At the conclusion of this chapter, you will be able to:

1. Define the term training, note its benefits, and discuss common obstacles to and myths about training.

2. Recognize basic learning principles that influence how training programs should be planned and implemented.

3. State characteristics that are important for an effective trainer.

4. Explain procedures required for use in the first seven steps in a formal training process:

    1. Define training needs
    2. Conduct a position analysis
    3. Define training objectives
    4. Develop training plans
    5. Develop training lessons
    6. Develop a training handbook
    7. Prepare trainees

Study Notes

The following is composed of important points from each chapter. Key terms are located in boxes for easy recognition.

1. Introduction to Training

    a. What is Training?
    b. Benefits of Training
    c. Obstacles of Training
    d. Training Myths

a. What is Training?

> **Training**: The process of developing a staff member's knowledge, skills, and attitudes necessary to perform tasks required for a position.

- Effective training is performance-based. It should be planned and delivered systematically to help trainees become more competent in the tasks that are essential for on-job performance.

> **Performance-based (training)**: A systematic way of organizing training in efforts to help trainees learn the tasks considered essential for effective on-job performance.

> **Cost effective**: A term that indicates that something such as training is worth more than it costs to provide it.

> **Competency**: Standards of knowledge, skills, and abilities required for successful job performance.

> **Feedback**: Response provided to a question or larger-scale inquiry such as a customer survey.

- The *morale* of staff members generally improves when they recognize their employer's interest in helping them to work in a way that best serves the organization and its guests.

> **Attitude**: Positive or negative feelings, beliefs, and values about something that influence a person to act in certain ways.

> **Morale**: The total of one's feelings about his or her employer, work environment, peers, and other aspects of the employment.

- Effective training programs address the knowledge and skills needed to perform basic job tasks. However, they cannot consider everything that may confront employees on the job.

b. Benefits of Training

- The numerous benefits to effective training include:

  - Improved performance. Trainees learn knowledge and skills to perform required tasks more effectively, and their on-job performance can be improved. They become value-added employees who can consistently achieve desired results.

- Reduced operating costs. Improved job performance helps reduce errors and rework, and associated costs can be reduced. Persons performing the job correctly will be more productive, fewer staff and/or labor hours will become necessary, and this, in turn, can help reduce labor costs.

- More satisfied guests. Training can yield staff members who are more service-oriented and who will know what their guests desire and require.

- Reduced work stress. Persons who can correctly perform the activities that are part of their positions will likely feel better about doing the job. Stress created by interactions with supervisors who are upset about improper work outputs, with peers who must take the time to do rework created by the employee's errors, and/or with frustrated guests about service and/or quality defects will be reduced.

- Increased job advancement opportunities. Who is most likely to be promoted to a more responsible and higher-paying position: a competent or an incompetent employee? Training can assist staff in attaining their promotion goals.

- Improved staff relationships. Persons who can do their jobs are more likely to work in a team effort, and all will do their fair share of required work in the correct way. Staff members who are trained to perform tasks beyond the scope of their normal position can also help peers in other positions.

- More professional staff. Professionals want to do their job as best they can, and this is only possible with appropriate training.

- Fewer operating problems. Busy managers can focus on priority concerns, and they will not need to address routine operating problems caused by inappropriate training.

- Lower turnover rates. Labor shortages confront most hospitality operators. Fewer new staff members become necessary as turnover rates decrease. Those who are properly trained and rewarded for successful performance are less likely to leave, and managers have less need to recruit new employees in increasingly tight labor markets.

- Increased morale. Training can help staff members feel good about themselves and their employers. These positive attitudes can have a significant influence on one's overall perceptions of the workplace.

- Higher levels of work quality. Effective training identifies quality standards that help define acceptable product and service outputs. Trained staff members are more interested in operating equipment correctly, in preparing the right products, and in properly interacting with guests.

- Easier to recruit new staff. Satisfied staff tell their family and friends about their positive work experiences, and their contacts may become candidates for

73

position vacancies that arise. Hospitality operations that emphasize training can evolve into employers of choice that provide first choice rather than last choice employment opportunities.

- Increased profits. It makes sense that, if guests are more satisfied and revenues increase and, if labor and other operating costs are reduced, there is a significant potential for increased profits. In the long run, training must be value-added. In other words, it must be worth more than it costs. This can be measured by the difference between the increased profits and the added training costs. While this measurement is not easy to make, most industry observers believe that, if training is done correctly, it will always win in the comparison.

Value-added: The concept that something is worth more than it costs, that output is consistently correct, and that behavior or the product is changed.

Turnover rate: The number of employees who leave an organization each year expressed as a percentage of the average number of workers employed by the organization.

Employer of choice: An organization with a reputation of offering a desirable place to work and with recruiting efforts made easier because of this perception.

---

c. Obstacles to Training

- Insufficient time for managers, supervisors, and/or trainers to plan for and deliver the training

- Too much time for trainees to be away from their positions to participate in the training

- Lack of financial resources to compensate for the trainer's and trainees' time and to acquire necessary training resources

- Insufficient trainers' knowledge and skills. Persons must be taught how to train, just as they must be taught to perform any other unfamiliar task.

- Lack of quality resources available for training. No manager or supervisor has the time, knowledge, and ability to develop training videos and/or to prepare extensive or sophisticated training resources or training evaluation tools. If these materials can't be developed in-house, are they available off-the-shelf? Resources addressing generic topics such as supervision tactics, sanitation, and safety can be purchased.

- Scheduling conflicts. When can front desk agents meet to learn a new way to perform a task? When can dining room servers be brought together for a group training session on guest service?

- Turnover. In many hospitality operations, some staff members leave within a few months (or less) of initial employment. Managers may think, "Why train employees if they don't remain on the job long enough to use what they have learned?" In fact, as noted previously, effective training can reduce turnover rates, and property managers who do not train are likely contributing to their unacceptably high turnover rate.

- Insufficient lead time between one's hire date and the time when he or she must be on the job. Hopefully, a warm-body syndrome is never used as a recruitment and/or selection tactic. Instead, staff are trained for expanded position duties, and recruitment tactics begin for new employees before an incumbent leaves and a position vacancy has occurred.

- Difficulty in maintaining training consistency. When individual trainers plan and deliver training activities based on what they think staff must know, the what and how of training may be inconsistent. Then those who train may begin to think that, "We tried to train, and it hasn't worked very well. There must be a better problem resolution alternative than training. What else can we do?"

- Trainer apathy. There should be reasons for trainers to want to train. Benefits for successful training duties can include special privileges, compensation increases, advancement consideration, educational opportunities, and/or recognition. By contrast, when trainers must assume these duties in addition to other tasks, if they do not receive train-the-trainer training and/or if there is no (or little) support for training, why should trainers want to do so?

> **Off-the-shelf**: Generic training materials, typically addressing general topics of concern to many trainers, that are available for use if company-specific resources are not available.

> **Warm-body syndrome**: The selection error that involves hiring the first person who applies for a position vacancy.

d. Training Myths

Myths (untruths) about training can create obstacles. Examples include:

- Training is easy. In fact, when training only involves a trainee tagging along with a more-experienced staff member, it is easy. However, the lack of planning and the increased possibility that basic training principles will be disregarded increases the likelihood that this type of training will be ineffective.

- Training costs too much. Hospitality operations with a history of inadequate training that has yielded unsatisfactory results are unlikely to invest the resources required to plan and deliver more effective training. "Been there; done that; let's try something else" is a philosophy that can easily evolve.

- Training is a staff function. Staff positions are manned by technical specialists who provide advice to, but do not make decisions for, people in chain-of-command line positions. Training is a line function that is too important to delegate to staff human resources personnel, if available, who may assist with recruitment, selection, and orientation tasks.

- Only new staff need training. New employees do need training, but so do their more-experienced peers when, for example, operating procedures are revised because of technology or when new equipment is purchased. Employees with a wide range of experience may also want to participate in professional development programs.

- There is no time for training. Many priorities compete for the limited time available to hospitality managers. In this context, training is often deemphasized, and available time is allocated to other tasks.

Professional development programs: Planned educational and/or training activities to prepare one for successively more responsible positions in an organization or industry.

---

2. Learning Principles Drive Training Principles

Learning Principles
- **Learning Principle 1:** Trainees Must Want to Learn and Need Motivation to Do So
- **Learning Principle 2:** Training Should Consider the Trainees' Life and Professional Experiences
- **Learning Principle 3:** Trainees Require Time to Learn
- **Learning Principle 4:** Trainees Should Know the Training Requirements
- **Learning Principle 5:** Training Should Consider the Trainees' Attention Spans
- **Learning Principle 6:** Learning Should Be Paced
- **Learning Principle 7:** Learning Speed Varies for Trainees

Training Principles
- **Training Principle 1:** Trainers Must Know How to Train

- **Training Principle 2:** Training Must Focus on Real Problems
- **Training Principle 3:** Training Must Emphasize Application
- **Training Principle 4:** Training Should Be Informal
- **Training Principle 5:** Training Should Employ a Variety of Training Methods
- **Training Principle 6:** Training Focus Should Be on Trainees
- **Training Principle 7:** Trainers Should Allow Trainees to Practice
- **Training Principle 8:** Trainers Require Time to Train
- **Training Principle 9:** Training Environment Must Be Positive
- **Training Principle 10:** Trainees Should Be Treated as Professionals
- **Training Principle 11:** Trainees Need Encouragement and Positive Feedback
- **Training Principle 12:** Trainees Should Not Compete Against Each Other
- **Training Principle 13:** Trainees Should Be Taught the Correct Way to Perform a Task
- **Training Principle 14:** Train One Task at a Time
- **Training Principle 15:** Train Each Task Using a Step-by-Step Plan

> **Jargon**: Terminology used by and commonly known only to persons who are familiar with a topic.

3. Focus on the Trainer

Here are twelve characteristics that are important for every good trainer:

- Have the desire to train. Good trainers want to train. There are several reasons why a trainer might desire to do so, including an interest in helping others, internal recognition for a job well done, and the knowledge that effective trainers are frequently promoted to higher-level positions within the department. Unfortunately, there are also reasons why training might not be an attractive assignment, including the expectation that the trainer must complete all regularly assigned tasks and also conduct training. Also, a trainer might want to do a good job but not be able to do so. This occurs when the staff member has not been taught how to train and/or because there is insufficient time, equipment, money, or other resources required to do so. Regardless of the reason, the resulting stress is a disincentive for the training assignment.

- Have the proper attitude about the employer, peers, position, and the training assignment. Hospitality organizations that emphasize the importance of staff members and that provide quality training opportunities to all employees at all levels will likely increase the morale of their trainers. Conversely, when training is just another and not-so-important responsibility, a less-than-willing attitude is likely.

- Possess the necessary knowledge and ability (skills) to do the job for which training is needed. Effective trainers must be knowledgeable about and have the skills necessary to perform the work tasks for which they will train others.

- Utilize effective communication skills. Trainers are effective communicators when they (1) speak in a language that is understandable to the trainee, (2) recognize that body language is a method of communication, (3) use a questioning process to learn the extent to which a trainee has learned, and (4) speak to communicate rather than to impress. For example, they don't use unfamiliar jargon, and they teach new staff members the meaning of unusual but commonly used terms.

- Know how to train. The importance of train-the-trainer programs should be obvious but often is overlooked.

- Have patience. Few trainees learn everything they must know or be able to do during their first exposure to training. Effective trainers have patience and understand that training steps must sometimes be repeated several times in different ways. They know that the goal is not to complete the training quickly; rather, it is to provide the knowledge and skills the trainee needs to be successful.

- Exhibit humor. Use of humor in good taste often provides a subtle message to a trainee: "I am enjoying the opportunity to provide training, and I hope you enjoy it as well. Learning can be fun, because the position is enjoyable."

- Have time to train. Effective training takes time, and it must be scheduled for the trainer and for the trainees.

- Show genuine respect for the trainees. This characteristic is driven by the need to treat trainees as professionals. You'll likely find that those whom you respect will also respect you. This mutual respect allows training to be more effective.

- Be enthusiastic. Newly employed staff members want reinforcement that their decision to join the organization was a good one. Initial experiences with an enthusiastic trainer help develop the foundation for successful training and for employees' long-term commitment. Trainers can reinforce the philosophy of more senior staff: "This is a good place to work: let's make it a better place to work, and this training will help us to do so."

- Celebrate the trainees' success. Have you ever heard the saying that, "If a trainee hasn't learned, it is because the trainer hasn't trained?" A successful trainer is one who has successfully trained, and the reverse is also true: trainers have not been successful when their trainees have not learned. Take time to celebrate when learning occurs.

- Value diversity. Increasingly, hospitality organizations employ persons with a variety of backgrounds and cultures, and the property is strengthened because of the different perceptions that provide input into decision making. All staff share the need to be well-trained. An effective trainer accepts the challenge to develop all trainees to the fullest extent possible, even though training tactics might differ based on the trainees' cultural backgrounds. For example, group trainers may need to actively solicit question responses from trainees who don't readily participate in discussions, and trainees from some cultures may be embarrassed to participate in role-play exercises.

> **Body language**: The gestures, mannerisms, expressions, and other nonverbal methods that people use to communicate with each other.

4. Use a Formal Training Process

Step 1: Define Training Needs
Step 2: Conduct a Position Analysis
Step 3: Define Training Objectives
Step 4: Develop Training Plans
Step 5: Develop Training Lessons
Step 6: Develop a Training Handbook (File)
Step 7: Prepare Trainees

Step 1: Define Training Needs

Training needs can be determined in several ways:

- Observation of work performance. Those who manage by walking around may note work procedures that deviate from required standard operating procedures. Note: Hopefully, the required procedures were taught in applicable training sessions!

- Input from guests. Successful managers attempt to learn about their guests' needs and the extent to which they are met. Surveys can help identify problems, and ongoing interactions with guests can also be helpful.

- Input from staff members. Some managers use suggestion boxes, open-door policies, and frank input from performance appraisals and coaching sessions to identify problems that can be resolved with training.

- Inspections. Formal inspections such as those related to safety and informal inspections made by supervisors and others before, during, and after work shifts can suggest revisions in work processes that lend themselves to training.

- Failure to meet performance standards. Consider, for example, unacceptable scores on visits by franchisor's representatives. Will training help address these concerns?

- Analysis of financial data. Differences between budget plans and actual operating data may suggest negative variances traceable to problems with training implications. Consider the many reasons that labor or other costs can be excessive. After problems are identified, corrective actions including training may be implemented.

- Performance/skills assessments. Post-training evaluation may suggest that the training provided has not been successful and that additional (or, at least, different) training is needed.

- Exit interviews. Formal or informal discussions with those who have resigned may identify training topics to help reduce turnover rates and to improve operations.

Step 2: Conduct a Position Analysis

- A position analysis identifies each task that is part of a position and explains how it should be done with a focus on knowledge and skills.

> **Position analysis**: A process that identifies each task that is part of a position and explains how it should be done with a focus on knowledge and skills.

- There are four basic steps in the position analysis process: (1) prepare a task list, (2) develop a task breakdown, (3) consider performance standards, and (4) write a position description.

> **Task list**: A list of all tasks that constitute a position.

> **Task breakdown**: A description of how one task in a task list should be performed.

> **Position description**: A human resources tool that summarizes a position and lists the primary tasks that must be performed as part of it.

> **Open-ended (question)**: A question that allows the respondent to elaborate on his or her response (e.g., What do you like about your job?).

- Procedures to develop a task list include:
  - Obtain interview input from the supervisors of and several experienced workers in the position being analyzed. Good interview questions are open-

ended (e.g., "Describe what you do in a normal work shift starting with when you begin work until you complete your shift."). More detailed interviews can include questions about the time spent on specific tasks, position responsibilities, instances of interaction with other staff, and the importance, frequency, and difficulty of performing specific tasks.

- Use available written information. Examples include position descriptions that provide a summary and an overview of tasks, existing task lists, and training materials used to teach new staff about their jobs.

- Use a simple questionnaire that asks, "What do you and others in your position do as part of your job?"

- Observe staff members as they work in their positions; compare what they actually do to the tasks they identified when questioned about their position responsibilities.

- If practical, work in the position(s) for which a task list is being developed.

> **Quality**: The essential characteristics consistently required for a product or service to meet the appropriate standard(s); a product or service attains necessary quality standards when the product or service is suitable for its intended purpose.

- When the position analysis process is correctly completed, tasks in each position (task list), how each task should be done (task breakdown), and quantitative and/or qualitative ways to determine if tasks are being done correctly (performance standards) will be known. As well, position descriptions will provide a handy way to reference and review the outputs of the position analysis process for managers, trainers, and staff.

Step 3: Define Training Objectives

Training objectives are used for two purposes:

1. To help the trainer connect the purpose(s) of the training program with its content. Specific reasons for training become clear when training needs are defined, and when the content of the training program is known after position analysis is undertaken.
2. To help evaluate training

- Training objectives specify what trainees should know and be able to do when they have successfully completed the training. Those who plan training programs must know what the training is to accomplish, and training objectives help planners to consistently do this.

81

Step 4: Develop Training Plans

Training plan: A description of the structure (overview) and sequence of the entire training program.

Several factors should be considered to determine the sequence for subject matter in the training plan:

- Begin with an introduction explaining why the training is important and how it will benefit the trainees.

- Provide an overview of training content.

- Plan training lessons to progress from simple to complex. Simple information at the beginning of the training will allow trainees to feel comfortable more quickly in the learning situation. It will also give them the confidence needed to master the program.

- Build on the trainees' experiences. Combine unfamiliar information with familiar content to allow trainees to build on their experience.

- Present basic information before more detailed concepts are discussed.

- Progress from general to specific.

- Consider the need for nice-to-know and need-to-know information. Basics should be presented before other information, and it is generally best to address the whys before the hows.

- Use a logical order. What information is prerequisite to other information as knowledge is developed or as skills are attained?

Step 5: Develop Training Lessons

Training lesson: The information to be presented in a single session of the training plan. Each lesson contains one or more specific training objectives and indicates the content and methodology(ies) required to enable trainees to master the content.

- Trainers can use a wide range of resources to develop training content including:
  1. Manufacturers' operating manuals for equipment
  2. Standard operating procedure manuals
  3. Task breakdowns for positions
  4. Applicable books and magazines including electronic editions

5. Industry best practices

6. Training resources from professional associations, such as the Education Foundation of the National Restaurant Association and the Education Institute of the American Hotel & Lodging Association

7. Materials available from suppliers

8. Ideas from other hospitality organizations

9. Notes taken by the trainer at other training sessions

10. The trainer's own experience

Step 7: Prepare Trainees

- Additional ways to motivate trainees to benefit from training include:

1. Tell trainees what to expect. The who, what, when, and where of training should be provided, specific questions should be addressed, and opportunities for group discussions about the training should be provided.

2. Explain why the training is needed. Whenever possible, state this in terms of what's in it for the trainees, rather than how it will benefit the property.

3. Provide time for the training. Effective training cannot be rushed, and it cannot be done during peak business times or whenever time is available. Dedicated time must be considered as schedules for trainers and trainees are developed.

4. Address trainees' concerns. For example, persons with language or reading problems and those wanting to know about the relationship, if any, between training and advancement opportunities have concerns to be addressed before the training begins.

5. Emphasize the importance of training. This factor is easy to accomplish in a property that supports training.

6. Explain that training will be directly related to the trainee's work. Coupled with a discussion about how trainees will directly benefit from the training, this will provide a powerful motivator for training acceptance.

7. Stress that the training will be enjoyable and worthwhile. This tactic should be easy to implement when the trainees have had positive experiences with past training efforts.

8. Tell the trainees how they will be evaluated. New staff will be looking for assurance that their employment decision was a good one. Experienced staff will know about the track record of their employer relative to the importance of training and the benefits derived from it.

Key Terms & Concepts Review: Quiz #1

This key terms and concepts quiz is designed to help you learn and better understand important chapter concepts and improve your Human Resources-related vocabulary.

Match the key terms with their correct definitions.

1. Training _____

2. Performance-based (training) _____

3. Cost effective _____

4. Competent _____

5. Task _____

6. Competency _____

7. Feedback _____

8. Attitude _____

9. Morale _____

10. Value-added _____

11. Turnover rate _____

12. Employer of choice _____

a. Positive or negative feelings, beliefs, and values about something that influence a person to act in certain ways.

b. Standards of knowledge, skills, and abilities required for successful job performance.

c. The total of one's feelings about his or her employer, work environment, peers, and other aspects of the employment.

d. A term that indicates that something such as training is worth more than it costs to provide it.

e. An organization with a reputation of offering a desirable place to work and with recruiting efforts made easier because of this perception.

f. The concept that something is worth more than it costs, that output is consistently correct, and that behavior or the product is changed.

g. A description that means the staff member has been appropriately trained and is able to contribute to the achievement of desired results.

h. The process of developing a staff member's knowledge, skills, and attitudes necessary to perform tasks required for a position.

i Generic training materials, typically addressing general topics of concern to many trainers that are available for use if company-specific resources are not available.

j. A systematic way of organizing training in efforts to help trainees learn the tasks considered essential for effective on-job performance.

k. The effective date that a new staff member begins work.

l. Response provided to a question or larger-scale inquiry such as a customer survey.

13. Off-the-shelf   _____   m.   A specific and observable work activity that is one component of a position and that has a definite beginning and end.

14. Hire date   _____   n.   The number of employees who leave an organization each year expressed as a percentage of the average number of workers employed by the organization.

Key Terms & Concepts Review: Quiz #2

This key terms and concepts quiz is designed to help you learn and better understand important chapter concepts and improve your Human Resources-related vocabulary.

Match the key terms with their correct definitions.

1. Warm-body syndrome _____

    a. A process that identifies each task that is part of a position and explains how it should be done with a focus on knowledge and skills.

2. Professional development programs _____

    b. A description of how one task in a task list should be performed

3. Jargon _____

    c. A description of the structure (overview) and sequence of the entire training program.

4. Body language _____

    d. The information to be presented in a single session of the training plan.

5. Position analysis _____

    e. A question that allows the respondent to elaborate on his or her response (e.g., What do you like about your job?).

6. Task list _____

    f. Planned educational and/or training activities to prepare one for successively more responsible positions in an organization or industry.

7. Task breakdown _____

    g. The selection error that involves hiring the first person who applies for a position vacancy.

8. Performance standards _____

    h. Measurable quality and/or quantity indicators that tell when a staff member is working correctly.

9. Position description _____

    i. Terminology used by and commonly known only to persons who are familiar with a topic

10. Open-ended (question) _____

    j. The gestures, mannerisms, expressions, and other nonverbal methods that people use to communicate with each other.

11. Training plan _____

    k. A human resources tool that summarizes a position and lists the primary tasks that must be performed as part of it.

12. Training lesson _____ l. A hard-copy or electronic manual (file) that contains the training plan and associated training lessons for a complete training program.

13. Training handbook _____ m. A list of all tasks that constitute a position.

14. Quality _____ n. The essential characteristics consistently required for a product or service to meet the appropriate standard(s); a product or service attains necessary quality standards when the product or service is suitable for its intended purpose.

Practice Quiz

To help you test your mastery of the chapter's content, choose the letter of the best answer to each of the questions listed below.

1. Training sessions called Professional Development are intended for:
    A. New, inexperienced employees
    B. New employees with some prior experience
    C. Owners and managers
    D. Existing employees
    Page 179

2. All of the following are examples of effective communication techniques EXCEPT:
    A. Recognizing the importance of body language
    B. Utilizing industry jargon
    C. Speaking to communicate rather than impress
    D. Using clear, understandable language
    Page 186

3. The most effective way to motivate employees during training is to:
    A. Allow new employees to decide if/when they would like to participate
    B. Always provide food
    C. Explain why the training is needed and what to expect
    D. Only require training of the most inexperienced hires
    Page 207

4. The following is NOT an effective way to identify training needs:
    A. Input from guests
    B. Inspections
    C. Wait for staff to assert their training needs
    D. Observation of work performance
    Page 190

5. The following is NOT generally considered a benefit of a good training program:
    A. Improved performance
    B. More satisfied guests
    C. Better staff relationships
    D. Improved staff relationships
    Pages 173-175

6. _____ is known as a process that identifies each task that is part of a position and explains how it should be done with a focus on knowledge and skills:
    A. Training plan
    B. Performance standard
    C. Task breakdown
    D. Position analysis
Page 191

7. The following is a MEASURABLE performance standard:
    A. Trainees will demonstrate a six-step method to manage guest complaints
    B. The Front Desk Agent should be able to check in guests as quickly as possible
    C. Trainees will realize the importance of effective guest service
    D. Trainees will understand the need to use a first-in first-out (FIFO) inventory rotation system.
Pages 196, 199-200

8. Good training programs include the following characteristics EXCEPT:
    A. Infrequent
    B. Personalized
    C. Conducted in the work place
    D. Paced for the employee
Pages 180-183

9. For the most part, performance-based training is best delivered:
    A. In a group-training session
    B. As one-on-one training
    C. Via the internet
    D. Performance-based training is not usually done for new employees
Page 173

10. The following is the most effective method for training new staff members:
    A. Reading information in a book
    B. Talking through a task
    C. Watching someone else perform a task
    D. Observation followed by hands-on practice
Page 183

For Your Consideration

Assume that, because of your HR background, you are called in to consult with a relatively large hospitality organization. The CEO of the company is concerned about potential discrimination charges. While a careful examination of the recruitment and selection procedures used by the company shows no bias for or against any protected employees group, the supervisors and middle managers of the company consist almost exclusively of members of only one race and gender.

After further discussion and some thorough investigation, you return to the CEO and present your findings. You suggest to the CEO that the company training program is the source of the problem. What is it that you likely found in the course of your investigation that would lead you to such a conclusion?

Chapter 7
Delivering and Evaluating Training Programs

Learning Objectives Review

At the conclusion of this chapter, you will be able to:

1. Provide an overview of the individual on-job training process.

2. Explain steps that are important in the four-step individual (on-job) training method:
    -   Preparation
    -   Presentation
    -   Trainee practice and demonstration
    -   Follow-up coaching

3. Explain additional on-job training approaches.

4. Provide an overview of the group training process.

5. Review specific procedures to prepare for group training:
    -   Group meeting room requirements
    -   Audiovisual requirements

6. Discuss procedures to facilitate group training:
    -   Presenting group training
    -   Interacting with group participants
    -   Conducting group training exercises
    -   Managing special training issues

7. Discuss the training evaluation process:
    -   Reasons for evaluation
    -   Levels of evaluation

Study Notes

The following is composed of important points from each chapter. Key terms are located in boxes for easy recognition.

1. Introduction to individual on-job training

- On-job training is commonly used in tourism and hospitality organizations. With this method, the trainer teaches job skills and knowledge to one trainee, primarily at the work station. Theoretically, it is the best type of training because it incorporates many learning and training principles.

> **On-job training**: An individualized (one-on-one) training approach in which a knowledgeable and skilled trainer teaches a less-experienced staff member how to perform tasks required for a position.

- On-job training can be supplemented by group training, and this tactic is especially useful when an operating problem affecting several staff members in a position must be addressed.

- On-job training can be easy. The steps involved in its planning and delivery are not complicated. However, the process does take time, and a commitment of financial resources is required to effectively plan and deliver it.

- There are several advantages to on-job training:

  - It incorporates basic adult learning principles.

  - It provides maximum realism. Training must focus on real problems, and these are encountered in the workplace.

  - It provides immediate feedback.

  - It can be used to train new and experienced staff.

  - It is frequently delivered by peers who regularly perform the task.

  - It is well accepted by trainees. This is an easy-to-understand point because it focuses on what's best for the trainee.

- Done correctly, there are few, if any, disadvantages to on-job training. Practiced the way it is in some tourism and hospitality organizations, however, several potential disadvantages can be cited:

  - Experienced staff members who have not learned how to train can make numerous errors while talking about and demonstrating proper performance.

- Training can be unorganized. Effective training should present a step-by-step approach.

- It can ignore the correct way to perform a task. When task breakdowns are not available or used, the trainer may teach the trainee how he or she does the work.

- It can create inappropriate work attitudes. Experienced staff members who know how and want to do their jobs correctly but do not know how to train can become frustrated with training responsibilities.

2. Steps in On-Job training

> **Preparation**: The first step in individualized (on-job) training, preparation involves all activities that must be done prior to the delivery of training.

> **Coaching**: A training and supervisory tactic that involves informal on-job conversations and demonstrations designed to encourage proper behavior and to discourage improper behavior.

Step 1: Preparation

- The following principles are useful when preparing for on-job training. Each will have already been addressed if the earlier steps in the training process noted in Chapter 6 were implemented.
  - State training objectives. Training objectives for the entire training program must be available in the training plan and for each segment of the training in training lessons.
  - Use/revise applicable task breakdown. A task breakdown explains how a task should be performed.
  - Consider the training schedule. The training plan should indicate how long the training activity will require, as well as where in the overall training sequence that dessert preparation training should occur.
  - Select training location. When practical, training should occur at the actual work station where the task will be performed.
  - Assemble training materials/equipment. The training lesson and supporting standard recipe should be in the training handbook.
  - Set up work station. The trainer should ensure that the work station is relatively free of anything that might detract from the training.
  - Prepare the trainee. A new staff member should know the purpose of initial training: to provide the knowledge and skills required to perform all tasks required for the position.

- Determine what the trainee already knows.

Step 2: Presentation

- The training lesson suggests that the training should occur in the storeroom, and begins with an overview of how the task should be performed. Then applicable activities are demonstrated.

> **Broken case**: A shipping container such as a case that contains less than the complete number of issue units (e.g., cans or bottles).

- The training lesson used is well-developed, so the task is divided into separate, teachable steps. The trainer explains the first step in the task, answers questions posed by the trainee, and then allows the trainee to repeat, practice, and/or demonstrate the step.

- As the presentation process evolves, the trainer follows several principles:
  - Speak in simple terms and do not use jargon.
  - When possible, present easier tasks before more complex activities.
  - Explain and demonstrate tasks slowly and clearly.
  - Use a questioning process to help assure trainee comprehension.
  - Emphasize the task breakdown as the training evolves. The trainer suggests that the trainee follow along using the task breakdown provided at the beginning of the training session.
  - Provide clear and well-thought-out instructions for each task. The trainer indicates why each step is necessary and why it should be done in a specific sequence.
  - Ask questions to help ensure that the trainee understands and to suggest when additional information, practice, or demonstration can be helpful.

Step 3: Trainee Practice and Demonstration

- The trainee should be asked to repeat or explain key points.
- The trainee should be allowed to demonstrate and/or practice the task. If practical, he or she should practice each step in the task a sufficient number of times to learn its basics before training continues.
- The trainer can use tactics to coach the trainee to reinforce positive performance (e.g., "Joe, you did that task flawlessly") and to correct improper

performance (e.g., "Andrew, you shouldn't have to look for the next item to be counted in the inventory because it is listed on the inventory sheet according to its storeroom location.")

- Trainers should recognize that, especially when the task and/or steps are difficult, initial progress may be slow.

- Trainers must realize that some trainees learn faster than others.

- Correct performance should be acknowledged before addressing performance problems. Some trainers refer to this as the sandwich method of appraisal.

- Trainees should be praised for proper performance. Everyone likes to be thanked for a job well done, to be told how important and special they are, and to receive immediate input about their performance.

Step 4: Coaching

- At the end of the training session, the trainee should be asked to perform, in sequence, each step in the task or step.

- The trainer should encourage questions.

- The trainer should provide ongoing reinforcement about a trainee's positive attitude and when the trainee improves his or her skills and knowledge.

- Close supervision immediately after training, and occasional supervision after a task is mastered, can help ensure that the trainee consistently performs the task correctly.

- Trainers should request that the trainee always perform the task correctly. Note: The trainer may ask the trainee about suggestions for other ways to perform tasks after the staff member has gained experience on the job.

- Trainees should be asked to retain copies of training materials provided during the session for later referral, if warranted.

3. Other Individual Training Methods

- Self-study. Trainees can enroll in distance education programs offered by a post-secondary educational institution or a professional association.

- Structured work experiences. A staff member may be assigned a specific project under the guidance of a mentor or more-experienced staff member to both learn and to assist the employer.

- Cross-training. This training method includes general activities that allow staff to learn tasks in another position.

- Job enrichment. Job enrichment occurs when a trainee learns tasks that are traditionally performed at a higher organizational level. This is sometimes called vertical job expansion.

- Job enlargement. This training opportunity occurs when additional tasks that are part of a position at one organizational level are added to another position at the same level. This is sometimes called horizontal job expansion.

- Job rotation. This training method involves the temporary assignment of persons to different tasks to provide work variety or experience. Like other individualized work methods, job rotation benefits the staff member and helps create backup expertise within the organization

> **Distance education**: An individual training method in which a staff member enrolls in a for-credit or not-for-credit program offered by a post-secondary educational facility or a professional association. Training can occur in a traditional manner, including use of hard-copy resources and examinations, or by more contemporary electronic education and training media.

> **Cross-training**: A training tactic that allows employees to learn tasks in another position.

> **Job enrichment**: This individual training method involves adding tasks to a position that are traditionally performed at a higher organizational level; also called vertical job expansion.

> **Job rotation**: The temporary assignment of persons to different positions or tasks to provide work variety or experience while creating backup expertise within the organization.

4. Introduction to Group Training

> **Group training**: A training method that involves presenting the same job-related information to more than one trainee at the same time.

- Two popular group training methods are used in tourism and hospitality organizations:

    1. Lecture. The trainer talks and may use audiovisual equipment or handouts to facilitate the session. Question-and-answer components may also be included.

2. Demonstration. The trainer physically shows trainees how to perform position tasks. Trainees can hear and see how something is done, often in the actual work environment.

Lecture (group training): A spoken presentation or speech made by a trainer to instruct a group of trainees.

Handouts: Hard-copy information applicable to the training topic that is given to trainees to help them learn a training concept.

Breakout (group training): A group training method in which all trainees are divided into small groups to complete selected training exercises. Groups may use a separate room or space within a single training room to conduct their activity.

5. Preparing for Group Training

    a. Training Room Requirements
    b. Audiovisual Requirements

a. Training Room Requirements

- Training rooms should be clean, well-ventilated, free from noisy distractions, and provide controlled room temperature.

- Proper table and chair arrangements help facilitate training. Front-of-room areas must allow space for all of the trainer's materials and equipment. This can include a table, lectern, flip chart(s), laptop computer, and digital projector (*if* PowerPoint overheads *will be used*). Other equipment needed can include a television monitor, videocassette recorder (VCR) or digital video disc (DVD) player (frequently on a mobile cart), screen (unless wall- or ceiling-mounted), overhead transparency projector, and other items necessary for demonstrations, handouts, or other needs. Trainers also appreciate ice water or another beverage, so tabletop space for this purpose is also required.

Full-service hotel: A lodging operation offering food and beverage services, including à la carte dining and banquet operations and, frequently, room service.

Limited-service hotel: A lodging property that offers no or limited food and beverage service. Many limited-service hotels offer a continental or other cold breakfast selection.

Flip chart: A pad of large paper sheets placed on a tripod or other stand that allows a trainer to write helpful training information.

PowerPoint overheads: Electronic overheads that are displayed on a screen with a digital projector using a disc or from a computer's hard drive.

Digital projector: A machine that converts image data from a computer or video source and projects it onto a screen for viewing.

b. Audiovisual Requirements

- Effective trainers use a variety of supplemental media to emphasize training points and to maintain the trainees' attention. Among the most popular audiovisual tools are flip charts, hard-copy overhead transparencies, videos, and PowerPoint overheads.

Brainstorming (group training): A method of group problem solving or alternative generation in which all group members suggest possible ideas.

6. Facilitating Group Training Sessions

      a. Trainer Presentation Skills
      b. Interacting with Group Participants
      c. Three Types of Trainees
      d. Conducting Group Training Exercises
      e. Managing Special Training Issues

a. Trainer Presentation Skills

- What is required is a planned, organized, and practiced approach to training delivery that avoids common public speaking mistakes. Trainers who have this foundation of public speaking skills will likely deliver an effective training session.

Ice breaker (training): A brief exercise facilitated at the beginning of a training session that allows trainees to meet each other, provides a transition from the job to the training environment, and generates enthusiasm about the training.

- Experienced trainers keep trainees tuned in to the session by providing methods for their active involvement and by asking open-ended questions of all trainees (not just of those who volunteer). They speak at the appropriate volume and pace. Trainers should avoid slang terms and jargon that hinder communication effectiveness. This is frequently a challenge because of the diverse group of employees in many organizations. Effective trainers pronounce words correctly, change voice tones, and avoid public speaking errors such as the frequent use of stalling expressions.

b. Interacting with Group Participants

- Trainers must attempt to get the trainees involved in their own learning process.
- Basic principles can help trainers guide discussions:

  1. Have an attitude of openness. Trainers should not be defensive and have to sell a training point. They should solicit questions, consider discussion feedback, and use it as a benchmark for assessing comprehension.

  2. Treat trainees as professionals (not subordinates). Successful tourism and hospitality organizations promote teamwork, and this is as important during training as at any other time.

  3. Ask clear and direct questions. The question, "Does everyone understand?" will not be as helpful as an open-ended question such as, "Why is it important to consider a guest's concern when addressing complaints?"

  4. Invite participants to make comments. Some trainees like to dominate the training. Others may be passive but able to contribute when requested to do so.

  5. Allow only one person to talk at a time. This rule is needed to show respect and is important to control the training environment.

  6. Listen carefully; show respect for all ideas. Trainers should listen to the remarks of everyone to understand what is being said. The common mistake of formulating a response while tuning out additional points must be avoided.

  7. Encourage more than one response. Effective trainers make trainees feel at ease and subtly encourage responses, including questions and comments from everyone.

  8. Don't be afraid of silence. If there is no response to a question, ask another one or use it to guide the next interaction: "Since there's no response, I'd like to repeat what I'm asking in another way."

  9. Keep the discussion focused. Using a training lesson is an excellent way to do this. Trainee discussions can be more difficult to guide, but an effective trainer knows when to steer the discussion back to the applicable topic: "That's an interesting idea, John. It would be great to discuss that, but we should focus on

inventory management right now to ensure that we'll have time to cover everything."

c. Three Types of Trainees

   1. Passive Trainees

   2. Dominating Trainees

   3. Disruptive Trainees

d. Conducting Group Training Exercises

- Creative trainers can utilize role-play, case study, and brainstorming exercises that allow trainees to more fully participate in and benefit from the training.

- Role-plays are group training exercises in which trainees pretend to be persons in situations addressed by the training who apply information presented in the training. Sometimes called dialog training, a role-play exercise can be very useful because it allows trainees to practice what they have learned in a risk-free situation.

- A case study allows trainees to study a real-world situation and to use what was learned in training to address the case study problem(s). Two examples of training content that could be supplemented with a case study are:

   1. An organization with high staff turnover rates could be described to determine what might be causing the problem.
   2. A budget and income statement could be shown. Follow-up analysis could allow trainees to determine where financial variances exist and to suggest what might be causing them.

- Brainstorming is a method of group problem solving or alternative generation in which all group members suggest possible ideas.

e. Managing Special Training Issues

- A wide range of important training issues should be considered because, regardless of how minor they appear, they can dramatically impact training outcomes:

   1. Be aware of personal mannerisms that can be annoying or distracting. A trainer's body language can distract trainees.

   2. Schedule training so applicable procedures can be implemented on a timely basis.

3. Effectively manage trainees who don't want to be trained.

4. Don't attempt to accomplish too much. Allow sufficient time for practice (skill training) and discussion (group training). Realize that training often takes longer than the planned time.

5. Listen to trainees. Be alert for trainee overload and side conversations, blank stares, and a preoccupation with non-training activities.

6. Be flexible. Change the training schedule when necessary. Be alert to the need to change training content, training location, or to use alternative training delivery formats to make the training more beneficial.

7. When applicable, field (pilot) test the training.

8. Use humor appropriately. It is difficult to prejudge one person's perspective of humor relative to many training topics, especially in a large group training session.

9. Keep the training on track of its stated objectives. This is easily done when training plans and lessons have been carefully developed and are consistently used.

10. Don't reinvent the wheel; if cost-effective materials are available, use them

11. Rehearse before training. Just as trainees must practice to learn a task, trainers should also practice to gain experience with their presentation. Be aware of appearance and hygiene.

12. Don't develop a trainer's ego. Remember that the objective of training is to improve the trainees' performance, not to impress trainees with the trainer's knowledge, skills, or experience.

13. Keep training sessions as short as possible. Experienced trainers know that several short training sessions are better than one relatively long one.

14. Recognize the importance of the training environment. Experienced trainers know that the environment of the meeting room is often more detrimental to training effectiveness than is the training content or its delivery.

15. Have backup contingencies for problems. Some problems such as inoperative audiovisual equipment and out-of-place training materials can be anticipated.

16. Respect the trainees' knowledge and experience. Wise trainers recognize that adult trainees bring a wide variety of personal experiences, attitudes, core values, and preconceptions to their training experience.

17. Link training to assessment and performance. Hopefully, training will show a cause-and-effect relationship.

18. Have fun! Trainees cannot learn if they do not enjoy their training. What is pleasurable to one trainee may not be for another. Using a variety of training

tactics that involve active trainee participation is preferable to less interactive approaches.

7. Training Evaluation

    a. Reasons to Evaluate Training
    b. Levels of Training Evaluation
    c. Training Evaluation Methods
    d. Follow-up Documentation

a. Reasons to Evaluate Training

- Assess the extent to which training achieved planned results. Training objectives have a two-fold purpose: (1) to identify competencies to be addressed in training, and (2) to provide a benchmark against which training can be evaluated.

- Identify strengths and weaknesses of training.

- Determine the success of individual trainees.

- Gather information to help justify future programs.

- Establish a database for future decisions.

- Determine trainees who are eligible for future training.

- Assess the costs and benefits of training.

- Reinforce major points for trainees.

- Assess trainees' reactions to training.

- Assess trainers' reactions to training.

b. Levels of Training Evaluation

- All training evaluation methods must meet at least five assessment criteria. The methods must be:

  - Valid. They must measure what they are supposed to measure.

  - Reliable. Training evaluation methods are reliable when they consistently provide the same results.

  - Objective. Objective evaluation methods provide quantitative (measurable) training assessments.

  - Practical. A training evaluation method is practical when the time and effort required for the assessment is worth its results.

- Simple. An evaluation method is simple when it is easily applied by the trainer, easily understood by the trainees, and when results are easy to assess and analyze by those evaluating the training.

Valid (training evaluation methods): Training evaluation methods that measure what they are supposed to measure.

Pretest/Post-test evaluation: A method used to evaluate training that involves administering the same test to trainees before (pretest) and after (post-test) the training. Positive differences in post-test scores provide an objective measure of training effectiveness.

- Effective trainers indicate in an introductory session that they will ask for feedback during the session.

- After-training evaluation can help assess whether training achieved its planned results. It may also identify how training sessions might be improved and assess the trainees' success.

c. Training Evaluation Methods

- Objective tests. These can be written, oral, and/or skill-based, and can be traditional written exams, oral assessments (utilizing open-ended questions), and/or after-training demonstrations.

- Observation of performance after training. Managers, supervisors, and trainers can manage by walking around and, in the process, note whether knowledge and skills taught during training are being applied. Storeroom personnel can be observed as they receive incoming products, and procedures used can be compared to those presented during training.

- Records of events (critical incidents). Assume there has been a theft of food products from a storage area after training in appropriate accounting and control procedures has been presented. Subsequent investigation determines that the recommended procedures were not used. The training program would not be considered effective, and staff with responsibilities to double-check as part of the inventory control process must, at the least, be retrained. Alternatively, procedures may need to be revised and followed with updated training in revised procedures.

- Self-reports.

- Interviews with trainees and/or trainers. The use of open-ended questions by trainers, managers, mentors, and/or human resources personnel may provide useful input about the training.

- Trainee surveys. Trainees can be questioned immediately after training, months after training, and/or during performance evaluation sessions about their training perspectives.

- Third-party opinions. Feedback from guests can help assess training that addressed aspects of products and service that affect them. The use of mystery shoppers in applicable types of hospitality operations is another example.

- Analysis of operating data. Training that addresses guest service and food costs should result in, respectively, increased guest service scores and lowered food costs if components of these data can be separated to determine how they were influenced by training.

- Exit interviews. Formal and informal conversations with employees who are leaving the organization can provide input that is helpful for training evaluation.

Critical incident: Any situation that identifies behaviors that contribute to success or failure on the job.

Manage by walking around: A management and supervision technique that involves a manager's presence in the workplace to determine if there are challenges that require corrective action, to praise staff for a job well-done, and to learn how and where one's management expertise, knowledge, and skills can best be utilized.

Mystery shopper: A person posing as a guest who observes and experiences an organization's products and services during a visit and who then reports findings to managers.

---

d. Follow-up Documentation

- Documentation is a final part of training evaluation. Training records to be maintained in the applicable staff member's personnel file include:
    - Name of trainee
    - Training dates
    - Training topics
    - Notes, if any, regarding successful completion
    - Other applicable information

Key Terms & Concepts Review: Quiz #1

This key terms and concepts quiz is designed to help you learn and better understand important chapter concepts and improve your Human Resources-related vocabulary.

Match the key terms with their correct definitions.

1. On-job training _____

2. Preparation _____

3. Coaching _____

4. Broken case _____

5. Closed-ended question _____

6. Sandwich method (performance appraisal) _____

7. Distance education _____

8. Cross-training _____

9. Underemployed (job status) _____

a. A tactic that involves praising an employee, suggesting an improvement tactic, and thanking the staff member for improvements made.

b. This individual training method involves adding tasks to a position that are traditionally performed at a higher organizational level; also called vertical job expansion.

c. A training tactic that allows employees to learn tasks in another position.

d. An individualized (one-on-one) training approach in which a knowledgeable and skilled trainer teaches a less-experienced staff member how to perform tasks required for a position

e. The condition that arises when a staff member is capable of working in a position with greater responsibilities than the position he or she currently occupies.

f. This individual training method occurs when additional tasks that are part of a position at the same organizational level are added to another position; also called horizontal job expansion.

g. The temporary assignment of persons to different positions or tasks to provide work variety or experience while creating backup expertise within the organization.

h. The first step in individualized (on-job) training, preparation involves all activities that must be done prior to the delivery of training.

i An individual training method in which a staff member enrolls in a for-credit or not-for-credit program offered by a post-secondary educational facility or a professional association.

10. Job enrichment   _____   j.   A shipping container such as a case that contains less than the complete number of issue units (e.g., cans or bottles).

11. Job enlargement   _____   k.   A training and supervisory tactic that involves informal on-the-job conversations and demonstrations designed to encourage proper behavior and to discourage improper behavior.

12. Job rotation   _____   l.   A question that can be answered with a "yes" or "no" response. Example: Do you like your job?

Key Terms & Concepts Review: Quiz #2

This key terms and concepts quiz is designed to help you learn and better understand important chapter concepts and improve your Human Resources-related vocabulary.

Match the key terms with their correct definitions.

1. Group training _____

2. Lecture (group training) _____

3. Handouts _____

4. Demonstration (group training) _____

5. Breakout (group training) _____

6. Full-service hotel _____

7. Limited-service hotel _____

8. Lectern _____

9. Flip chart _____

10. PowerPoint overheads _____

a. A training method in which the trainer shows trainees how to perform all or part of a task.

b. A lodging operation offering food and beverage services, including à la carte dining and banquet operations and, frequently, room service.

c. A lodging property that offers no or limited food and beverage service. Many limited-service hotels offer a continental or other cold breakfast selection.

d. Electronic overheads that are displayed on a screen with a digital projector using a disc or from a computer's hard drive.

e. A floor stand or tabletop unit, usually with a slanted top, used to hold the trainer's teaching materials.

f. A spoken presentation or speech made by a trainer to instruct a group of trainees.

g. A group training method in which all trainees are divided into small groups to complete selected training exercises. Groups may use a separate room or space within a single training room to conduct their activity.

h. A pad of large paper sheets placed on a tripod or other stand that allows a trainer to write helpful training information.

i. A training method that involves presenting the same job-related information to more than one trainee at the same time.

j. Hard-copy information applicable to the training topic that is given to trainees to help them learn a training concept.

Practice Quiz

To help you test your mastery of the chapter's content, choose the letter of the best answer to each of the questions listed below.

1. The temporary re-assignment of a job task for the purpose of providing work variety and experience is called _____.
    A. Job enrichment
    B. Job enlargement
    C. Job rotation
    D. Training
Page 229

2. A "valid" training evaluation means that it:
    A. Consistently provides the same results
    B. Provides measurable training assessments
    C. Measures what it is supposed to measure
    D. Is easily applied
Page 249

3. All of the following are examples of the third-party opinion method of training evaluation EXCEPT:
    A. Mystery shoppers
    B. Managing by walking around
    C. Comment cards
    D. Follow-up interviews with guests
Page 253

4. The following is LEAST likely to be utilized when engaging the demonstration method of group training:
    A. Discussion
    B. Role plays
    C. Case study analysis
    D. Lecture
Pages 230-231

5. At this step of the training process it is most appropriate to correct substandard performance:
    A. Coaching
    B. Trainee practice and demonstration
    C. Trainee presentation
    D. Trainee preparation
Page 223

6. When a trainee _____ job enrichment occurs.
   A. Learns tasks traditionally performed at a higher organizational level
   B. Learns tasks in another position
   C. Completes the training process
   D. Graduates from a training program and assumes trainer responsibilities
Page 228

7. The FIRST step in the individual on-job training method is:
   A. Trainee preparation
   B. Trainee practice and demonstration
   C. Coaching
   D. Trainee presentation
Page 219

8. The following is NOT an important principle for effective trainers:
   A. Always fill moments of silence
   B. Ask clear and direct questions
   C. Keep the discussion focused
   D. Invite participants to make comments
Page 240

9. _____ is a good way to observe and evaluate whether knowledge
   and skills taught during training are being applied after training is complete.
   A. Managing by walking around
   B. Objective tests
   C. Have the trainees fill out and evaluation
   D. Training self-assessment forms
Pages 250-251

10. The following is an advantage of on-job training:
   A. It eliminates the need for a training handbook
   B. Experienced employees already know the skills necessary to train
   C. It is expensive
   D. It provides immediate feedback
Page 217

For Your Consideration

Evaluating the success of a skills-training program can be fairly easy. In such a situation, employees can, upon having completing the training, readily be observed to have acquired, or not to have acquired, the skill which the training was designed to impart.

Evaluating the effects of attitudinal training can be more difficult. Assume that you designed and implemented a training program whose purpose was to improve the quality of "Guest Service" among a group of hotel front desk agents. After the training has been delivered, what specific techniques could you employ to evaluate how effective your program was in actually improving the "Guest Service" provided by the newly trained front desk agents?

Chapter 8
Compensation Programs

Learning Objectives Review

At the conclusion of this chapter, you will be able to:

1. Describe the differences between extrinsic and intrinsic rewards as they relate to employee compensation programs.

2. Explain how compensation programs are affected by federal, state, and local laws.

3. List and describe the most common forms of direct financial compensation.

4. List and describe the most common forms of indirect financial compensation.

5. List and describe some of the most common forms of non-financial compensation.

Study Notes

The following is composed of important points from each chapter. Key terms are located in boxes for easy recognition.

1. Compensation Management

> **Compensation**: The amount of money and other items of value (e.g., benefits, bonuses, perks) given in exchange for work performed.

> **Compensation package**: The sum total of the money and other valuable items given in exchange for work performed.

- When less-skilled workers are attracted to an organization, and when the best of an organization's workers ultimately seek employment elsewhere, customer service levels inevitably are below average, resulting in below-average company profits.

- The optimum compensation program attracts very high-quality workers, provides for excellent customer service levels, and, by doing so, allows the company to maximize profitability.

Extrinsic rewards: Financial, as well as non-financial, compensation granted to a worker by others (usually the employer).

Intrinsic rewards: Self-initiated compensation (e.g., pride in one's work, a sense of professional accomplishment, or enjoying being part of a work team).

- It is important to recognize that not all employees react in the same manner to rewards offered by employers. For some workers, intrinsic rewards are critically important. For others, financial rewards may be most important, and for still others, status and the non-financial extrinsic rewards may be what they like most about the compensation they receive.

- The goal of any effective compensation management program should be to attract, motivate, and retain competent employees. To achieve this goal, the program must be perceived by employees as essentially fair and equitable.

Compensation management: The process of administrating an organization's extrinsic and intrinsic reward system.

- Those HR managers who can clearly show employees the inherent fairness of their company's complete compensation program will, in the long run, attract and retain the best workforce. This is so because compensation directly affects employee motivation, and motivation affects employees' view of compensation.

- Effective compensation system typically includes:
    1. Categorizing of jobs.
    2. Comparison of employee pay to the local labor market.
    3. Management of internal pay equity.
    4. Linkage of pay to job performance.
    5. Maintenance of open communications.

Pay range: The lower and upper limit of hourly wages or salary paid for a specific job. For example, the pay range for an entry-level room attendant in a hotel may be between $7.50 and $8.50 per hour to start.

> **Local wage rate**: The prevailing pay range for distinct job categories in a specific community or labor market.
>
> **Salary survey**: A comprehensive review of local wage rates and pay ranges paid for one or more individual job categories (e.g., the average local wage rate, or range, paid to hotel bartenders, room attendants, or groundskeepers).

> **Merit pay system**: A compensation program that links increases in pay to measurable job performance. Under such a system, those workers who perform better receive proportionally larger percentage pay increases.

2. Legal Aspects of Compensation Management

> a. Federal Legislation
> b. State Legislation
> c. Local Legislation

a. Federal Legislation

> **Minimum wage**: The least amount of wages that employees covered by the FLSA or state law may be paid by their employers.

- The minimum wage is established and periodically revised by Congress. It's most recent revision occurred in 2007. HR managers would do well to continually monitor the actions of Congress with regard to changes in the minimum wage, because nearly all hospitality employees are covered by the minimum wage, with some exceptions.

b. State Legislation

- Many states continue to maintain their own minimum wage laws. In those states, employees are covered by the law that is most favorable to them (in other words, whichever wage [state or federal] that provides the highest compensation).

c. Local Legislation

- In many cases, this local legislation takes the form of living-wage laws that, in most cases, can directly affect hospitality businesses.

> **Living wage**: The minimum hourly wage necessary for a person to achieve some subjectively defined standard of living. In the context of developed countries such as the United States, this standard is generally considered to require that a person working 40 hours per week, with no additional income, should be able to afford a specified quality or quantity of housing, food, utilities, transportation, and health care.

- As a final word on the legal aspects of compensation, it is important to note that employers may (voluntarily) commit themselves to the legal responsibility to pay workers a specific amount. Thus, for example, when an employer agrees, in writing, to pay one of its executives $100,000 per year, it is legally obligated to do so. In a similar manner, an organization that agrees to specific wage rates in a union contract must pay those rates to employees covered by the contract.

3. Direct Financial Compensation

    a. Salaries
    b. Wages
    c. Incentives and Bonuses
    d. Tips

a. Salaries

> **Salary**: Pay calculated on a weekly, monthly, or annual basis rather than at an hourly rate.

- The advantage to employees of a salary system is the consistency of their pay. An advantage to employers is that such employees are not subject to the overtime provisions of the FLSA.

> **Exempt (employee)**: An employee who is not subject to the minimum wage or overtime provisions of the Fair Labor Standards (FLSA).

> **Nonexempt (employee)**: An employee who is subject to the minimum wage or overtime provisions of the Fair Labor Standards (FLSA).

- Several widely publicized lawsuits have been filed against companies in the hospitality industry that violated salary provisions of the FLSA. As a result, it is important that HR managers understand the federal provisions related to salary payments. They must also remember that, when the state laws regarding salary payments differ from the FLSA, an employer must comply with the standard that is most protective (beneficial) to the salaried employee.

b. Wages

- In the hospitality industry, wages paid to workers typically take the form of hourly wages or piecework wages.

Hourly wages: Money paid or received for work performed during a one-hour period.

Piecework wages: Money paid or received for completing a certain amount (one piece) of work.

- It should be easy for most HR managers to understand that, while a true piecework wage system may be intended to minimize the time it takes for room attendants to do their jobs, in addition to other disadvantages, such a system as currently applied in hospitality also encourages employees to hurry through their work and, as a result, speed rather than room cleanliness is rewarded.

c. Incentives and Bonuses

Performance-based pay: A compensation system that rewards workers for their on-job accomplishments rather than for time spent on the job.

Incentive: Motivational plan provided to employees based on their work efforts.

Bonus: Financial reward paid to employees for achieving predetermined performance goals.

- When designed carefully, performance-based pay components can increase worker income and lead directly to improvements in guest service and product quality levels

- When incentives are tied to specific aspects of job performance, some workers may avoid performing unmeasured, and thus unrewarded, activities in favor of measured and rewarded activities.

d. Tips

> **Tip**: A gift of money given directly to someone for performing a service or task. Also known as a gratuity.

- If an employee's hourly tip earnings (averaged weekly) added to this hourly wage do not equal the minimum wage, and then the employer is responsible for paying the difference between the minimum wage and the *tip* credit amount.

> **Tip credit**: The amount of tips employers are allowed to count (credit) toward the wage payments they make to employees.

- HR managers should remember that the Department of Labor will also allow employers whose employees are tipped on a credit (or debit) card to reduce the payment card tips by an amount equal to the handling charges levied by the payment card company.

> **Tip-pooling**: An arrangement in which service providers share their tips with each other on a predetermined basis.

> **Service charge**: An amount added to a guest's bill in exchange for services provided.

4. Indirect Financial Compensation
   a. Mandatory Benefits
   b. Voluntary Benefits
   c. Other Voluntary Benefits

> **Benefits (employee):** Indirect financial compensation offered to attract and keep employees or to comply with legal mandates.

> - **Mandatory benefits (employee):** Indirect financial compensation that must, by law, be offered to employees.

> - **Voluntary benefits (employee):** Indirect financial compensation a company chooses, on its own, to offer its workers in an effort to attract and keep the best possible employees.

a. Mandatory Benefits

- Most experts estimate that government-mandated benefits such as social security, workers' compensation, and unemployment insurance represent approximately 10 percent of an employer's total payroll cost.

- At the federal level, the government's mandatory social security program is an insurance program funded through a dedicated payroll tax.

- At the state level, workers' compensation now provides medical and disability benefits for work-related injuries and illnesses. In addition, all states mandate an employer's participation in a workers' unemployment insurance program.

b. Voluntary Benefits

- Each organization must determine what it feels is the best set of benefits to offer. In many cases, the answer to this question is determined by the type of worker employed, the profitability of the company, and the operational philosophy of the employer.

- A variety of health insurance programs can be offered by employers, including:
    - Medical insurance.
    - Prescription drug plans.
    - Dental plans.
    - Vision care plans.

AD&D insurance: Short for Accidental Death and Disability, a form of life and income replacement insurance.

Payroll deduction: A payment method in which the employer deducts money from an individual employee's paycheck and submits it directly to a program (e.g., insurance, savings, or retirement) in which the employee participates. These deductions may be made from an employee's after-tax or pretax wages.

- An additional and popular income protection plan is a short-term disability, or pay continuance, program. Typically, these plans offer income continuance that provides the employee with full pay for the first month of disability, and then provides a benefit that ranges from 50 to 75 percent of the employee's pay for up

c. Other Voluntary Benefits

- Paid time-off.: Companies spend approximately 10 percent of payroll on paid time-off plans.
- Holidays. The paid holidays that virtually every company provides are New Year's Day, Memorial Day, Independence Day (July 4), Labor Day, Thanksgiving Day, and Christmas Day.
- Vacation days. Paid vacation granted to, usually, only full-time employees, often varies with years of service.
- Sick pay. Sick or personal days are paid time-off for employee illness. Most companies also allow employees to use these days for the illness of a family member.
- Retirement programs. Retirement plans typically cost organizations about 3 to 5 percent of payroll. These are most often offered as either a pension plan or a 401(k) plan. Pension plans are typically funded only by the company.
- Employee Assistance Plans (EAP). These programs provide counseling for employees encountering a variety of life issues.
- Health Care Reimbursement Accounts (HCRA) and Dependent Care Reimbursement Accounts (DCRA). These programs allow certain medical expenses, deductibles, and child care costs for employees and their families to be paid by employees on a pretax basis.
- Hospitality-specific benefits. By the very nature of their businesses, some hospitality companies can offer their employees benefits such as reduced-cost meal programs, hotel stays, or travel. Discounted dining, guest rooms, and transportation offered at greatly reduced employee rates are very popular employee benefits and can usually be offered by employers at a relatively low cost.

5. Nonfinancial Compensation

- Some of the most common and effective of the intrinsic motivators used in the hospitality industry provide employees with:
    - Increased participation in decision making
    - Greater job freedom
    - More responsibility
    - Flexible work hours
    - Opportunities for personal growth
    - Diversity of tasks

- Many experienced HR managers believe that an organization's ability to communicate the rationale behind its compensation programs is just as important as the quality of the programs. Organizations that maximize the effectiveness of their overall compensation programs often find that clear communication of the program's processes and objectives helps them to achieve employee recruitment and retention goals established for the programs.

Key Terms & Concepts Review: Quiz #1

This key terms and concepts quiz is designed to help you learn and better understand important chapter concepts and improve your Human Resources-related vocabulary.

Match the key terms with their correct definitions.

1. Compensation _____

2. Compensation package _____

3. Extrinsic rewards _____

4. Intrinsic rewards _____

5. Compensation management _____

6. Pay range _____

7. Salary survey _____

8. Merit pay system _____

9. Minimum wage _____

a. The process of administrating an organization's extrinsic and intrinsic reward system.

b. A comprehensive review of local wage rates and pay ranges paid for one or more individual job categories (e.g., the average local wage rate, or range, paid to hotel bartenders, room attendants, or groundskeepers).

c. The minimum hourly wage necessary for a person to achieve some subjectively defined standard of living. In the context of developed countries such as the United States, this standard is generally considered to require that a person working 40 hours per week, with no additional income, should be able to afford a specified quality or quantity of housing, food, utilities, transportation, and health care.

d. A compensation program that links increases in pay to measurable job performance. Under such a system, those workers who perform better receive proportionally larger percentage pay increases.

e. The amount of money and other items of value (e.g., benefits, bonuses, perks) given in exchange for work performed.

f. Self-initiated compensation (e.g., pride in one's work, a sense of professional accomplishment, or enjoying being part of a work team).

g. Money paid or received for work performed during a one-hour period.

h. An employee who is subject to the minimum wage or overtime provisions of the Fair Labor Standards (FLSA).

i Pay calculated on a weekly, monthly, or annual basis rather than at an hourly rate.

10. Living wage _____ j. The sum total of the money and other valuable items given in exchange for work performed.

11. Salary _____ k. The lower and upper limit of hourly wages or salary paid for a specific job.

12. Hourly wages _____ l. An employee who is not subject to the minimum wage or overtime provisions of the Fair Labor Standards (FLSA).

13. Exempt (employee) _____ m The least amount of wages that employees covered by the FLSA or state law may be paid by their employers.

14. Nonexempt (employee) _____ n Financial, as well as non-financial, compensation granted to a worker by others (usually the employer).

Key Terms & Concepts Review: Quiz #2

This key terms and concepts quiz is designed to help you learn and better understand important chapter concepts and improve your Human Resources-related vocabulary.

Match the key terms with their correct definitions.

1. Piecework wages _____
2. Performance-based pay _____
3. Incentive _____
4. Bonus _____
5. Tip _____
6. Tip-pooling _____
7. Tip credit _____
8. Service charge _____
9. Benefits (employee): _____
10. Mandatory benefits (employee): _____

a. Financial reward paid to employees for achieving predetermined performance goals.

b. The amount of tips employers are allowed to count (credit) toward the wage payments they make to employees.

c. Indirect financial compensation offered to attract and keep employees or to comply with legal mandates.

d. An arrangement in which service providers share their tips with each other on a predetermined basis.

e. Money paid or received for completing a certain amount (one piece) of work.

f. Motivational plan provided to employees based on their work efforts.

g. Indirect financial compensation that must, by law, be offered to employees.

h. A compensation system that rewards workers for their on-job accomplishments rather than for time spent on the job.

i. Indirect financial compensation a company chooses, on its own, to offer its workers in an effort to attract and keep the best possible employees.

j. A retirement plan that allows employees in private companies to make contributions of pretax dollars to a company pool that is then invested for them in stocks, bonds, or money market accounts.

11. Voluntary benefits (employee)   _____   k. A payment method in which the employer deducts money from an individual employee's paycheck and submits it directly to a program (e.g., insurance, savings, or retirement) in which the employee participates. These deductions may be made from an employee's after-tax or pretax wages.

12. AD&D insurance   _____   l. An amount added to a guest's bill in exchange for services provided.

13. Payroll deduction   _____   m. A gift of money given directly to someone for performing a service or task. Also known as a gratuity.

14. 401(k) (retirement) plan   _____   n. Short for Accidental Death and Disability, a form of life and income replacement insurance.

Practice Quiz

To help you test your mastery of the chapter's content, choose the letter of the best answer to each of the questions listed below.

1. The following is an example of an extrinsic reward:
    A. Empowerment
    B. Voluntary Benefits
    C. Job Freedom
    D. Job Security
Page 266

2. In 1994 the first living-wage law was passed in _____.
    A. New York, New York
    B. Portland, Oregon
    C. Baltimore, Maryland
    D. Los Angeles, California
Page 273

3. The legal guidelines of the FLSA states that tips received by employees may be counted as wages for up to _____ of the minimum wage:
    A. 10%
    B. 25%
    C. 35%
    D. 50%
Page 280

4. An example of a hospitality specific benefit would be:
    A. Social Security
    B. 401-K
    C. Vision Care Plan
    D. Discounted employee hotel room rates
Page 287

5. Intrinsic rewards are essential because they do which of the following:
    A. Make an employee's work more meaningful
    B. Show appreciation of employees
    C. Create a more cohesive work environment
    D. All of the above
Pages 256, 288-289

6. Which of the following is NOT a form of direct financial compensation?
    A. Salaries
    B. Bonuses
    C. Tips
    D. Employee discounts
Pages 275-276

7. This step might include conducting a salary survey during the development of a
    compensation system
    A. Management of internal pay equity
    B. Categorizing of jobs
    C. Linkage of pay to job performance
    D. Comparison of employee pay to the local labor market
Pages 267-268

8. The term "exempt" when referring to an employee, means that the employee:
    A. Is not required to submit to a background check
    B. Is not subject to the minimum wage or overtime provisions of the FLSA
    C. Is not entitled to paid time-off
    D. Is not eligible for benefits
Page 276

9. If the minimum wage at a hospitality operation is $7.00 per hour and the allowable tip
    credit is 50%, the overtime rate to be paid would be:
    A. $3.50
    B. $7.75
    C. $7.00
    D. $10.50
Page 281

10. Which of the following is an example of an intrinsic reward?
    A. Profit Sharing
    B. Tips
    C. Personal Growth
    D. Meal Discounts
Page 266

For Your Consideration

One of the most difficult challenges faced by HR professionals assigned to administer compensation programs relates to the establishment of international pay scales. For those companies that operate units in several countries, complex decisions related to fairness in compensation programs are the rule, not the exception.

Part of the difficulty in such a situation relates to the fact that the range of pay in many foreign countries is much narrower than in the U.S. Thus, for example, a departmental manager in a full-service hotel located in the U.S. might earn $80,000 per year, while the same department head in one of the company's London properties might earn the equivalent of $100,000. However, the U.S. hotel's General Manager might earn $200,000 with bonus, while the GM of the London property earns $150,000. HR managers often struggle when addressing how, in this situation, a company-wide compensation program could be structured that will satisfy the department head who earns less than his foreign counterpart, while at the same time fairly compensating the London GM who earns less than her U.S. counterpart.

Assume you were responsible for proposing a management pay scale that would be used in all of your company's international units and regions. In addition to addressing range of pay, what other issues would you need to address if such a program were to be viewed as "fair" by those affected by it?

Chapter 9
Performance Management and Appraisal

Learning Objectives Review

At the conclusion of this chapter, you will be able to:

1. Identify the benefits of a formal performance appraisal program.

2. Explain the rationale for each of the four steps in a progressive disciplinary program:

   - Documented oral warning
   - Written warning
   - Suspension
   - Dismissal

3. Describe the role of employee improvement tactics as an integral part of the performance management process.

4. Differentiate between a voluntary and a nonvoluntary employee separation, and explain the function of the exit interview.

5. Identify major legal issues related to performance management and appraisal.

Study Notes

The following is composed of important points from each chapter. Key terms are located in boxes for easy recognition.

1. Performance Management

a. Overview of Performance Appraisal
b. Common Performance Appraisal Methods
c. Other Performance Appraisal Methods and Issues

- Effective hospitality managers provide ongoing performance feedback to their employees. This process is integral to maximizing the effectiveness of an operation's workforce.

> **Performance management**: A systematic process by which managers help employees to improve their ability to achieve goals.

> **Appraisal (employee)**: An objective and comprehensive rating or evaluation of employees.

- Performance appraisal is the employee evaluation component of a performance management process. An effective process yields clear employee goals and an objective rating of goal attainment.

a. Overview of Performance Appraisal

- Performance goals set by supervisors and employees. Goals can be short- or long-term and address numerous issues. They should be specific and quantifiable where possible.
- Regular, informal feedback from supervisors. Annual formal appraisals do not allow employees to assess progress toward goal attainment. More frequent input is needed, which occurs as supervisors work closely with employees and provide them with ongoing coaching.
- A formal method to address performance or disciplinary problems. Methods used to correct inadequate job performance should be known, fair, and applied equally to all employees.
- Regular and formal appraisal. Formal reviews that accurately document each staff member's performance should be conducted regularly. In addition to pinpointing improvement concerns, appraisals should identify specific steps for employees to enhance their long-term position with the organization.

b. Common Performance Appraisal Methods

- A properly implemented formal performance appraisal system yields many benefits:
    - Recognition of outstanding performance.
    - Identification of necessary improvements.
    - Clarification of work standards.
    - Opportunity to analyze and redesign jobs.
    - Identification of specific training and development needs.
    - Determine professional development activities.
    - Validation of screening and selection processes.
    - Opportunity for employee feedback and suggestions.
    - Objective method to identify candidates for pay increases and promotion.

Customers (internal): Employees of the hospitality operation.

Customers (external): Guests served by the hospitality operation.

Absolute standard (performance appraisal method): Measuring an employee's performance against an established standard.

Examples of absolute standard evaluation methods include:

- Critical incident. Critical incidents are those specific behaviors essential (critical) to doing a job successfully.
- Checklist appraisal. Yes or no responses are used to address behavioral factors applicable to the successful completion of tasks identified in a job description.
- Continuum appraisal. This approach uses a scale to measure employee performance relative to specific factors.
- Forced-choice appraisal. This appraisal method is a special checklist in which the evaluator must choose between two (or more) alternative statements that describe two (or more) opposing choices.

Relative standard (performance appraisal): Measuring one employee's performance against another employee's performance.

Targeted outcome (performance appraisal): Measuring the extent to which specified goals were achieved.

BARS: Short for Behaviorally Anchored Rating Scales, an appraisal system in which employees are evaluated based on their display of definitive, observable, and measurable behaviors.

BOS: Short for Behavioral Observation Scale, a type of appraisal system in which judgments about employee performance are related to a series of statements describing specific examples of observable behaviors.

Goal setting and goal achievement measurements and rewards are not new concepts. Management by objectives (MBO), the concept of using identifiable objectives to measure performance and to assign employee rewards, is decades old.

c. Other Performance Appraisal Methods and Issues

- While performance appraisal is primarily a managerial task, employees can play a valuable role in their own performance evaluations.

Peer evaluation: An appraisal system that utilizes the opinions of coworkers to evaluate an employee's performance.

Upward assessments (appraisal system): An appraisal system that utilizes input from those staff members who are directly supervised by the staff member being evaluated.

360-degree appraisal (performance appraisal system): A method of performance appraisal that utilizes input from supervisors, peers, subordinates, and even guests and others to provide a comprehensive evaluation of a staff member's performance.

Halo effect: The tendency to let the positive assessment of one individual trait influence the evaluation of other, nonrelated traits.

Pitchfork effect: The tendency to let the negative assessment of one individual trait influence the evaluation of other, nonrelated traits.

2. Progressive Discipline
   a. Documented Oral Warning
   b. Written Warning
   c. Suspension
   d. Dismissal

Discipline (management action): Any effort designed to influence an employee's behavior.

Disciplined (workforce description): The situation in which employees conduct themselves according to accepted rules and standards of conduct.

- Positive discipline is used to encourage desired behavior, while negative discipline is used to discourage improper behavior. Both human resources and supervisory personnel should be concerned about the proper use of a property's discipline efforts.

> **Progressive discipline**: A program designed to modify employee behavior through a series of increasingly severe punishments for unacceptable behavior.

a. Documented Oral Warning

> **Documented oral warning**: The first step in a progressive discipline process: a written record is made of an oral reprimand given to an employee.

- The written record of an oral warning should include the employee action that preceded the warning, the date of the incident and of the oral warning, and the name of the supervisor issuing the reprimand.

b. Written Warning

> **Written warning**: The second step in a progressive discipline process that alerts an employee that further inappropriate behavior will lead to suspension.

- The written warning step must be done correctly to protect the organization if the employee later challenges the legitimacy (legality) of the progressive disciplinary process.

- It is a good rule to praise in public and to reprimand in private. However, many progressive discipline processes require an observer to be present at the second and later steps in the process. Co-managers, supervisors, or others can monitor the discussion and serve as an eyewitness.

c. Suspension

> **Suspension**: The third step in a progressive discipline process: a period off from work resulting from ongoing inappropriate behavior.

- An action to suspend an employee must be documented, and the information should be placed in the employee's permanent file. Some employees may refuse to sign the document. Despite an employee's view that an unsigned document will somehow invalidate it, this refusal carries virtually no meaning if the employee had the opportunity to sign it. If an employee refuses to sign a discipline report, then the observer should sign the document and note the employee's refusal to do so.

d. Dismissal

- Dismissal is the final step in the progressive discipline process and should only be implemented for serious infractions.

- From an employee's perspective, dismissal means that even after repeated warnings, the organization's behavioral norms were not met. From the employer's perspective, dismissal means that the manager was unable to persuade the employee to modify his or her behavior sufficiently to maintain the job.

3. Behavior Improvement Tactics

a. Reinforcement of Appropriate Behavior
b. Elimination of Unacceptable Behavior

a. Reinforcement of Appropriate Behavior

- When managers encourage employees to perform in specific ways and the employees can do so, the desired behavior is reinforced, and it will occur more frequently. Even when the employee cannot perform a task, enthusiastic encouragement can cause performance improvement.

- Examples of specific tactics to reinforce positive behavior include:
    - Saying more than "thank you" or "good job." The best managers encourage specific behaviors.
    - Doing it on the fly. The best managers do not wait to encourage employees until it is less hectic.
    - Telling them directly. Managers may tell those around them how much they appreciate an employee, but they sometimes feel uncomfortable telling that employee directly.
    - Meaning what is said. A manager's tone of voice, eye contact, and body language can enhance or detract from a message.
    - Putting it in writing. Encouraging words need not be typed and formal. A short, handwritten note is fast and easy. A complimentary note from one's boss can be shared proudly with family members and friends. A written

compliment is a source of pride to nearly every employee and demonstrates the power of recognition.

b. Elimination of Unacceptable Behavior

- When employees exhibit unwanted behavior, it is usually because they don't know the desired behavior, know it but do not know how to perform it, or know it and do not want to perform it.

Counseling (employee): A process to assist employees in overcoming performance problems.

- In some cases, undesirable employee performance may result from forces beyond his or her control. Financial difficulties, marital traumas, family emergencies, death of parent, spouse or child, substance abuse, and legal issues are examples of factors that can negatively affect performance.

4. Employee Separation

   a. Voluntary Separation
   b. Involuntary Separation
   c. Exit Interviews

Turnover: The replacement of one employee by another

- Some turnover is inevitable and is good for a business, because new staff members with diverse attitudes and ideas can be recruited. However, excessive turnover rates are detrimental to an operation's ability to maintain quality standards and costs and, sometimes, to remain financially viable.

a. Voluntary Separation

Voluntary (separation): An employee-initiated termination of employment.

- While these employee-initiated separations are often inconvenient, they rarely cause significant replacement issues. In the best-case scenario, the employee will inform managers about the pending departure in enough time that a replacement can be recruited and trained.

b. Involuntary Separation

- Involuntary employment separations are frequently caused by poor employee performance. However, management may also have failed to properly select, orient, train, and direct the work of these employees.

> - **Involuntary (separation)**: An employer-initiated termination of employment.

- Significant increases in payments to employees who are involuntarily separated will result in an increase in the amount the employer must pay into the state's unemployment compensation accounts.

c. Exit Interviews

- Exit interviews are typically utilized when an employee voluntarily resigns. Then HR managers ask questions while taking notes, or request that the employee complete a questionnaire or a short survey.

5. Legal Considerations of Performance Management and Appraisal

  a. Title VII of the Civil Rights Act
  b. Equal Pay Act
  c. Americans with Disabilities Act
  d. Age Discrimination in Employment Act

a. Title VII of the Civil Rights Act

- Title VII of the Civil Rights Act (1964) specifically prohibits employers from using non-job-related factors for employee evaluation, promotion, or termination.

> **Protected class**: A group of workers with a characteristic specifically identified by an employment-related law or ordinance as protected.

b. Equal Pay Act

- The Equal Pay Act (1963) requires equal pay for men and women doing equal work, if the jobs performed require equal skill, effort, and responsibility, and if they are performed under similar working conditions.

c. Americans with Disabilities Act

- The Americans with Disabilities Act (ADA) affects the hiring of workers in this protected class, and it also directly affects the manner in which managers evaluate workers with disabilities. The Act prohibits managers from considering disability when evaluating worker performance.

d. Age Discrimination in Employment Act

- The Age Discrimination in Employment Act (ADEA) prohibits organizations with 20 or more employees from treating workers aged 40 and older differently (including in the areas of appraisal and performance management) from other workers based on their age.

Key Terms & Concepts Review: Quiz #1

This key terms and concepts quiz is designed to help you learn and better understand important chapter concepts and improve your Human Resources-related vocabulary.

Match the key terms with their correct definitions.

1. Performance management   _____   a.   Measuring an employee's performance against an established standard.

2. Appraisal (employee)   _____   b.   Measuring the extent to which specified goals were achieved.

_____   c.   A plan developed by an employee and his or her supervisor that defines specific goals, tactics to achieve them, and corrective actions, if needed.

3. Customers (internal)

4. Customers (external)   _____   d.   A systematic process by which managers help employees to improve their ability to achieve goals.

5. Absolute standard (performance appraisal method)   _____   e.   Short for Behaviorally Anchored Rating Scales, an appraisal system in which employees are evaluated based on their display of definitive, observable, and measurable behaviors.

6. Measuring an employee's performance against an established standard.   _____   f.   An objective and comprehensive rating or evaluation of employees.

7. Targeted outcome (performance appraisal)   _____   g.   Employees of the hospitality operation.

8. BARS   _____   h.   An appraisal system that utilizes input from those staff members who are directly supervised by the staff member being evaluated.

9. BOS   _____   i   The ability of a measuring tool to yield consistent results.

10. Management by objectives   _____   j.   An appraisal system that utilizes the opinions of coworkers to evaluate an employee's performance.

11. Peer evaluation   _____   k.   Measuring one employee's performance against another employee's performance.

12. Upward assessments (appraisal system) _____ l. The ability of a measuring tool to evaluate what it is supposed to evaluate.

13. 360-degree appraisal (performance appraisal system) _____ m. Guests served by the hospitality operation.

14. Reliability (measurement tool) _____ n. The tendency to let the positive assessment of one individual trait influence the evaluation of other, non-related traits.

15. Validity (measurement tool) _____ o. A method of performance appraisal that utilizes input from supervisors, peers, subordinates, and even guests and others to provide a comprehensive evaluation of a staff member's performance.

16. Halo effect _____ p. Short for Behavioral Observation Scale, a type of appraisal system in which judgments about employee performance are related to a series of statements describing specific examples of observable behaviors.

Key Terms & Concepts Review: Quiz #2

This key terms and concepts quiz is designed to help you learn and better understand important chapter concepts and improve your Human Resources-related vocabulary.

Match the key terms with their correct definitions.

1. Pitchfork effect _____

a. Any action designed to correct undesirable employee behavior.

2. Discipline (management action) _____

b. The third step in a progressive discipline process: a period off from work resulting from ongoing inappropriate behavior.

3. Disciplined (workforce description) _____

c. The first step in a progressive discipline process: a written record is made of an oral reprimand given to an employee.

4. Discipline (positive) _____

d. The replacement of one employee by another.

5. Discipline (negative) _____

e. The tendency to let the negative assessment of one individual trait influence the evaluation of other, nonrelated traits.

6. Progressive discipline _____

f. Any action designed to encourage proper behavior.

7. Documented oral warning _____

g. An employer-initiated separation of employment.

8. Reprimand _____

h. Any effort designed to influence an employee's behavior.

9. Written warning _____

i. An employee-initiated termination of employment.

10. Suspension _____

j. The second step in a progressive discipline process that alerts an employee that further inappropriate behavior will lead to suspension.

11. Dismissal _____

k. A meeting between a representative of the organization and a departing employee.

12. Counseling (employee) _____

l. The situation in which employees conduct themselves according to accepted rules and standards of conduct.

13. Turnover _____

m. A process to assist employees in overcoming performance problems.

14. Voluntary   _____   n. The honest intent to act without taking an unfair
    (separation)   advantage over another person.

15. Involuntary   o. A program designed to modify employee
    (separation)   behavior through a series of increasingly severe
                                     punishments for unacceptable behavior.

16. Exit interview   p. A formal criticism or censure by a person with
                                     authority to do so.

17. Good faith   q. An employer-initiated termination of
                                     employment.

Practice Quiz

To help you test your mastery of the chapter's content, choose the letter of the best answer to each of the questions listed below.

1. All of the following should be done in an effective employee appraisal system EXCEPT:
    A. Identify and correct employee weakness
    B. Emphasize employee's negative characteristics
    C. Reinforce employee strengths
    D. Plan work and set expectations
Page 297

2. The appraisal system that is an example of an absolute standard appraisal method is:
    A. Group Order Ranking
    B. Critical Incident
    C. Management by Objectives
    D. Individual Order
Page 303

3. Management by Objectives is an example of a(n):
    A. Absolute standard appraisal method
    B. Relative standard appraisal method
    C. 360-degree appraisal method
    D. Targeted outcomes appraisal method
Page 307

4. A performance appraisal method is said to be _____ when it delivers consistent and dependable measurements:
    A. Valid
    B. Fair
    C. Reliable
    D. Absolute Standard
Page 308

5. Performance goals should be set by:
    A. Supervisors and employees
    B. Supervisors
    C. Investors
    D. Entry-level employees
Page 297

6. An example of an internal customer would be:
    A. A customer at a fast food restaurant's drive-thru window
    B. A motel's night auditor
    C. A patron of a local coffee shop
    D. A long-term stay customer at a hotel
Page 300

7. The following is a characteristic NOT defined as a protected class according to Title VII of the Civil Rights Act:
    A. Gender
    B. Sexual Orientation
    C. Age
    D. Religion
Page 322

8. _____ is the first step in a progressive disciplinary system:
    A. Written warning
    B. Suspension
    C. Dismissal
    D. Documented oral warning
Page 310

9. Behaviorally Anchored Rating Scales are a form of_____:
    A. Individual Order Appraisal
    B. Targeted Outcome Appraisal
    C. Checklist Appraisal
    D. None of the above
Page 306

10. A systematic process by which managers help employees to improve their ability to achieve goals is called.
    A. Performance appraisal
    B. Performance management
    C. A critical incident
    D. The halo effect
Page 296

For Your Consideration

In large hospitality organizations, HR managers are often called upon to participate in progressive discipline sessions. The role of the HR specialist may be to ensure that company policies are followed, or simply to serve as a witness to counseling sessions. In smaller hospitality units, the manager/ HR specialist are one and the same individual, thus progressive discipline sessions may be the sole responsibility of that manager.

Regardless of a unit's size, however, progressive discipline programs should be designed (among other goals), to ensure the appropriateness of worker's on-the-job behaviors. However, not all managers and supervisors (especially those newly promoted to their jobs) will know exactly what is considered to be inappropriate workplace behavior. Assume you were charged with providing new supervisors with a list of "inappropriate" workplace behaviors for which employees should be "written up." What specific behaviors would you want to ensure are on your list?

Chapter 10
Employee Health and Safety

Learning Objectives Review

At the conclusion of this chapter, you will be able to:

1. Explain the roles of the two most important federal agencies responsible for ensuring employees are safe at work and are protected from those who would illegally harass them.

2. Explain the advantages enjoyed by employers who provide healthy worksites for their employees.

3. Describe the differences and similarities between employee assistance programs and employee wellness programs.

4. Review the legal and moral responsibilities employers have to ensure a safe and secure worksite for their employees.

5. List and describe specific steps employers can take to help prevent workplace violence.

Study Notes

The following summary includes many of the important points found in this chapter. Key terms are boxed for easy recognition.

1. Legal Aspects of Employee Protection
   a. Occupational Safety and Health Act
   b. Civil Rights Act of 1964 re: Harassment

a. Occupational Safety and Health Act

> **OSHA**: Short for the Occupational Safety and Health Administration, the agency responsible for enforcing the Occupational Safety and Health Act.

- Concerned about worker safety and health, the U.S. Congress passed the Occupational Safety and Health Act in 1970. It heralded a new era in the history of public efforts to protect workers from harm on the job. The Act established, for the first time, a nationwide, federal program to protect almost the entire workforce from job-related death, injury, and illness.

- OSHA's current role is to ensure the safety and health of America's workers by setting and enforcing standards; providing training, outreach, and education; establishing partnerships; and encouraging continual improvement in workplace safety and health.

- The work of OSHA has been a tremendous success. Since the enforcement agency created by this law began its work, occupational deaths have been cut by 62 percent, and injuries have declined by 42 percent.

- Currently, the major areas of OSHA-mandated record keeping related to the hospitality industry include:

  - Log and summary of all recordable injuries and illnesses.
  - Personal protective equipment (assessment and training).
  - Control of hazardous energy (lock out/tag out).
  - Hazard communication standards.
  - Emergency action plans and fire prevention plans.

b. Civil Rights Act of 1964 re: Harassment

- In 1980, the Equal Employment Opportunities Commission (EEOC) issued regulations defining sexual harassment and stating that it was a form of sexual discrimination prohibited by the Civil Rights Act of 1964. In 1986, the U.S. Supreme Court first ruled that sexual harassment was a form of job discrimination—and held it to be illegal.

- Employees can face a variety of harassment forms. These include:

  - Bullying. Harassment that can occur on the playground, in the workforce, or any other place.

  - Psychological harassment. This is humiliating or abusive behavior that lowers a person's self-esteem or causes them torment.

  - Racial harassment. The targeting of an individual because of his or her race or ethnicity.

  - Religious harassment. Verbal, psychological, or physical harassment used against targets because they choose to practice a specific religion.

  - Stalking. The unauthorized following and surveillance of an individual, to the extent that the person's privacy is unacceptably intruded upon, and the victim fears for his or her safety.

- Sexual harassment. This harassment can happen anywhere but is most common in the workplace (and schools). It involves unwelcome words, deeds, actions, gestures, symbols, or behaviors of a sexual nature that make the target feel uncomfortable.

2. Employee Health

- If worker productivity is reduced because workers cannot function properly at their jobs due to constant headaches, watering eyes, nausea, or fear of exposure to elements that can cause long-term health problems, then the entire industry and its guests will suffer. Consequently, maintaining a healthy work environment benefits the hospitality organization, its workers, and its customers.

- HR managers concerned about the health of their workers should directly address the following issues:
    - Provide sufficient quantities of fresh air.
    - Provide a smoke-free environment.
    - Keep air ducts clean and dry.
    - Maintain effective equipment inspection programs.
    - Monitor repetitive movement injuries.
    - Monitor stress levels.
    - Make lifesaving equipment and training readily accessible.
    - Pay attention to workers' complaints.

3. Employee Assistance Programs (EAPs)

a. Employee Wellness Programs

Wellness programs (employee): An employer-sponsored initiative designed to promote the good health of employees.

- Typical examples of employer-initiated wellness programs include the topics of quitting smoking, nutrition and weight management, high blood pressure control, weight loss, self-defense, exercise, and stress management. In many cases, employers who provide these programs find that their employees stay healthier and that the business's health insurance carriers offer discounts for implementation of these programs.

145

4. Employee Safety and Security

  a. Employee Safety Programs
  b. Crisis Management Programs

- From the perspective of an HR manager working in hospitality, safety can be considered a condition that minimizes the risk of harm to workers, while security relates to employees' feelings of fear and anxiety.

Safety: Freedom from the conditions that cause personal harm.

Security: Freedom from fear and anxiety related to personal harm.

Crisis: A situation that has the potential to negatively affect the health, safety, or security of employees.

---

a. Employee Safety Programs

- From a legal perspective, a hospitality operation's basic obligation is to act responsibly in the face of threats. One way to analyze and respond to those responsibilities is illustrated by the four-step, simplified system.

    Step 1: Recognition of the safety threat.
    Step 2: Program development in response to the threat.
    Step 3: Program implementation. .
    Step 4: Program evaluation.

b. Crisis Management Programs

- Because guests, as well as facilities, are typically affected in a crisis, hospitality managers in all functional areas should develop plans to deal with the potential for calamities they cannot prevent. As previously pointed out, in many small hospitality operations, the general manager may be responsible for a crisis response and for anticipating and managing the ways it will directly affect the employees.

- To prepare effectively for a crisis, HR managers should develop and practice emergency plans. An emergency plan identifies a likely crisis situation and then details how the operation will respond to it. After it is developed, an emergency plan must be practiced, so all employees will know what they should do during the crisis and when they should do it.

> **Evacuation plan**: The specific actions to be taken by managers and staff when vacating a building in response to a crisis.

- It is important to commit emergency plans to writing. This is crucial for two reasons: (1) a written plan will clarify precisely what is expected of management, as well as employees, in times of crisis; and (2) if the operation is involved in a lawsuit, the written emergency plan can serve as evidence to support its defense.
- Experiencing a crisis, especially one that entails injury or loss of life, can be very stressful. Negative effects on employees can include anxiety, depression, nightmares, flashbacks, and even physical effects such as insomnia, loss of appetite, and headaches. Collectively, these and related symptoms are known as post-traumatic stress disorder (PTSD).

5. Employee Security Programs

    a. Zero-Tolerance Harassment Programs
    b. Preventing Workplace Violence

a. Zero-Tolerance Harassment Programs

- The EEOC expects employers to affirmatively act to prevent all types of harassment. HR managers need to understand that the Meritor Savings Bank case ruling by the Supreme Court also addressed different standards for determining liability in cases of hostile environment *and* quid pro quo sexual harassment.

> **Hostile work environment (sexual harassment)**: A workplace infused with intimidation, ridicule, and insult that is severe or pervasive enough to create a seriously uncomfortable or abusive working environment with conduct severe enough to create a work environment that a reasonable person would find intimidating (hostile).

> **Quid pro quo (sexual harassment)**: *Quid pro quo* literally means "something for something." Harassment that occurs when a supervisor behaves in a way or demands actions from an employee that forces the employee to decide between giving in to sexual demands or losing her or his job, losing job benefits or promotion, or otherwise suffering negative consequences.

- For general guidelines in preventing harassment of all types, all HR managers should understand:
  - What is, and isn't, a hostile work environment.

- The company policy.
- The impact on unions.
- The effect of speech.
- Proper investigations.
- Personal liability.

- In all cases, a company will be held liable for a hostile work environment created by its workers if it knew (or should have known) that the harassment was occurring and it did not take reasonable action to stop it. Thus, a swift and appropriate resolution of harassment complaints is the best way to ensure a secure work environment and to protect your company from liability
- Managers should use zero-tolerance harassment policies to take action even for offensive conduct that does not meet the legal standard of a harassing environment. The reason is that even mild forms of harassment that go unchecked can disrupt an operation through decreased morale and productivity and increased employee turnover.

b. Preventing Workplace Violence

Workplace violence: Any act in which a person is abused, threatened, intimidated, or assaulted in his or her place of employment.

Implicit (threat): A threatening act that is implied rather than expressly stated. For example, the statement: "I'd watch my back if I were you!" said in a menacing voice by one employee to another.

Explicit (threat): A threatening act that is fully and clearly expressed or demonstrated, leaving nothing merely implied. For example, the statement: "If I see you in my work area again, I'll personally throw you out of it!" said in a menacing voice by one employee to another.

- Managers should understand that workplace violence is not limited to incidents that occur within a traditional workplace. Work-related violence can occur at off-site business-related functions such as conferences and trade shows, at social events related to work, and in clients' offices or away from work but resulting from work (e.g., a threatening telephone call from an employee to another employee's home or cell phone).
- At the very least, an effective workplace violence policy will detail:

- What specific behaviors (e.g., swearing, intimidation, bullying, harassment, and the like) management considers inappropriate and unacceptable in the workplace
- What employees should do when incidents covered by the policy occur
- Who should be contacted when reporting workplace violence incidents (including a venue for reporting violent activity by one's immediate supervisor)
- That threats or assaults that require immediate attention should be reported to the property's security department (if applicable) or directly to the police at 911

- While these points will cover the basic minimum of a workplace violence policy, the best workplace violence prevention policies will:
  - Be developed by management and employee representatives.
  - Apply to management, employees, customers, clients, independent contractors, and anyone who has a relationship with the operation.
  - Define exactly what is meant by workplace violence in precise, concrete language.
  - Provide clear examples of unacceptable behavior.
  - State in clear terms the operation's view toward workplace violence and its commitment to preventing workplace violence.
  - Precisely state the consequences of making threats or committing violent acts.
  - Encourage the reporting of all incidents of violence.
  - Outline the confidential process by which employees can report incidents and to whom.
  - Ensure that no reprisals will be made against those employees reporting workplace violence.
  - Outline the procedures for investigating and resolving complaints.
  - Describe how information about potential risks of violence will be communicated to employees.
  - Commit to provide support services to victims of violence.
  - Describe an active and effective Employee Assistance Program (EAP) to allow employees with personal problems to seek help.
  - Demonstrate a commitment to monitor and regularly review the policy.
  - Describe any regulatory or union-related requirements related to the policy (if applicable).

Key Terms & Concepts Review: Quiz #1

This key terms and concepts quiz is designed to help you learn and better understand important chapter concepts and improve your Human Resources-related vocabulary.

Match the key terms with their correct definitions.

1. OSHA _____   a. Nerve damage resulting in a burning, tingling, or itching numbness in the palm of the hand and the fingers, especially the thumb and the index and middle fingers.

2. Zero tolerance _____   b. Freedom from the conditions that cause personal harm.

3. Carpal tunnel syndrome _____   c. An employer-sponsored initiative designed to promote the good health of employees.

4. Automated external defibrillator (AED) _____   d. A situation that has the potential to negatively affect the health, safety, or security of employees.

5. Wellness programs (employee) _____   e. Freedom from fear and anxiety related to personal harm.

6. Security _____   f. A portable electronic device that can audibly prompt and deliver an electric shock that, in many cases, can increase survival rates of those suffering cardiac arrest.

7. Safety _____   g. Short for the Occupational Safety and Health Administration, the agency responsible for enforcing the Occupational Safety and Health Act

8. Crisis _____   h. The specific actions to be taken by managers and staff in response to a crisis.

9. Emergency plan _____   i. A policy that permits no amount of leniency regarding harassing behavior.

Key Terms & Concepts Review: Quiz #2

This key terms and concepts quiz is designed to help you learn and better understand important chapter concepts and improve your Human Resources-related vocabulary. Match the key terms with their correct definitions.

1. Evacuation plan _____ a. Harassment that occurs when a supervisor behaves in a way or demands actions from an employee that forces the employee to decide between giving in to sexual demands or losing her or his job, losing job benefits or promotion, or otherwise suffering negative consequences.

2. Post-traumatic stress disorder (PTSD) _____ b. Any act in which a person is abused, threatened, intimidated, or assaulted in his or her place of employment.

3. Hostile work environment (sexual harassment) _____ c. A severe reaction to an event that caused a threat to an individual's physical or emotional health

4. Quid pro quo (sexual harassment) _____ d. The typical, or average, person (and their behavior and beliefs) placed in a specific environmental setting.

5. Reasonable person (standard) _____ e. The specific actions to be taken by managers and staff when vacating a building in response to a crisis.

6. Workplace violence _____ f. A threatening act that is fully and clearly expressed or demonstrated, leaving nothing merely implied. For example, the statement: "If I see you in my work area again, I'll personally throw you out of it!" said in a menacing voice by one employee to another.

7. Implicit (threat) _____ g. A workplace infused with intimidation, ridicule, and insult that is severe or pervasive enough to create a seriously uncomfortable or abusive working environment with conduct severe enough to create a work environment that a reasonable person would find intimidating (hostile).

8. Explicit (threat) _____ h. A threatening act that is implied rather than expressly stated. For example, the statement: "I'd watch my back if I were you!" said in a menacing voice by one employee to another.

151

Practice Quiz

To help you test your mastery of the chapter's content, choose the letter of the best answer to each of the questions listed below.

1. Occupational deaths have_____ since the enactment of OSHA legislation.
    A. Increased by 5%
    B. Decreased by approximately 60%
    C. Stayed approximately the same
    D. Decreased by 5%
Page 334

2. A lock out/tag out standard regulates training and procedures as it relates to:
    A. Hazardous chemicals
    B. Fire prevention
    C. Unexpected machine movements
    D. Mechanical irritants
Page 338

3. _____will most likely constitute harassment of a sexual nature:
    A. Unauthorized following of an individual
    B. Unwelcome touching
    C. Humiliating behavior that lowers self-esteem
    D. Psychological harassing behavior
Page 339

4. The court determines if a workplace setting should be deemed as a "hostile environment" by apply _____.
    A. Zero-tolerance standards
    B. Quid pro quo definitions
    C. Reasonable person standards
    D. Employee assistance programs
Page 352

5. According to the Civil Rights Act of 1964 which of the following is NOT considered a form of harassment?
    A. All are considered forms of harassment
    B. Bullying
    C. Stalking
    D. Psychological harassment
Page 339

6. Which of the following can be the site of work-place violence?
    A. A client's office
    B. An organizational trade show
    C. Work holiday party
    D. All can be the site of work-place violence
Page 356

7. Which of the following is an example of an implicit threat?
    A. "If I see you in my work area again, I'll throw you out!"
    B. "I'd be pretty careful if I were you; accidents have a way of happening around here!"
    C. Throwing objects
    D. Hitting or shoving
Page 356

8. At hospitality businesses that have gone 100% smoke-free:
    A. Revenue levels have decreased
    B. Revenue levels have stayed the same or increased
    C. The effects are impossible to measure
    D. No hospitality businesses have gone 100% smoke-free to date
Page 341

9. The main objective of OSHA legislation is:
    A. To provide health care for all citizens
    B. To provide health care for all workers
    C. To provide health care for children
    D. To prevent work-related injuries, illnesses and deaths
Page 334

10. _____ is a concern that "Right to know" laws and regulations would address:
    A. Potentially hazardous chemicals
    B. Negligent hiring
    C. The content of personnel files
    D. The outside-work conduct of employees
Page 335

For Your Consideration

Typical examples of employer-initiated assistance programs related to wellness include those that address quitting smoking, nutrition and weight management, high blood pressure control, weight loss, self-defense, exercise, and stress management. In many cases, employers who provide these programs find that their employees stay healthier and that the business's health insurance carriers offer discounts for implementation of these programs. They are a win-win situation for employees and employers.

Assume you were responsible for proposing new areas that could be addressed by your company's own EAP. What specific areas of employee assistance (in addition to those wellness programs mentioned above) do you feel would be of most help to today's hospitality employees and as a result, to your own company?

Chapter 11
Role of Human Resources in Strategic Planning and Organizational Change

Learning Objectives Review

At the conclusion of this chapter, you will be able to:

1. Identify factors that influence organizational change, and discuss how they impact the role of human resources in managing it.

2. Explain the role of the human resources function in strategic planning.

3. Review the continuum of organizational change, and the role of the human resources function to manage change along it.

4. Explain basic issues that create organization-wide resistance to change, and explore human resources aspects of these issues.

Study Notes

The following summary includes many of the important points found in this chapter. Key terms are boxed for easy recognition.

1. Organizational Change Is Constant

> **Organizational change**: The process by which an organization moves away from what it is currently doing toward some desirable future status.

External influences:
- Legislation.
- Competition.
- Consumer preferences.
- Niche marketing:
- Demographic issues.
- Global issues.
- Ethical concerns.
- Economy.
- Employee unions.

Niche marketing: The activity of offering specific products and services to sub segments of a market in efforts to attract large numbers of this sub segment to the operation.

Strategy: A general method or plan developed in efforts to attain a long-range goal.

Tactic: A specific action step used to help attain a short-term objective.

2. Human Resources and Strategic Planning

a. Close Look at Strategic Planning Process
b. Summary of Strategic Planning Process

Strategic planning: A systematic method of developing long-term plans to attain business objectives by anticipating and adapting to expected changes.

a. Close Look at Strategic Planning Process

- Steps for strategic planning to consider appropriate dynamic change, with an emphasis on the human resources implementations.

    - Step 1: Consider the organization's mission.
    - Step 2: Scan the environment.
    - Step 3: Analyze the situation. (SWOT analysis; strengths, weaknesses, opportunities, and threats, is a popular method used to address the current situation confronting an organization).
    - Step 4: Determine long-term goals.
    - Step 5: Establish strategies.
    - Step 6: Identify interim objectives.
    - Step 7: Assign responsibilities and timelines.
    - Step 8: Communicate the plan.
    - Step 9: Monitor the plan; take corrective action as needed.
    - Step 10: Celebrate a successful plan.
    - Step 11: Repeat the planning process.

SWOT analysis: Strengths, Weaknesses, Opportunities, and Threats Analysis—a systematic approach to assess an organization's current environment as part of the strategic planning process.

> **Rolling plan (long-range planning)**: A plan in which the final year in the planning cycle is moved ahead one year as plans for each year are implemented.

b. Summary of Strategic Planning Process

- Human resources managers are integral members of their organization's top-leadership team. In this capacity, they represent and should be able to communicate the abilities of existing staff to accomplish reasonable plans, and to suggest the need for additional, perhaps more specialized, personnel to help the organization move forward in its goal attainment efforts.

3. Continuum of Change

a. Two Basic Types of Change
b. Role of Human Resources in Change

a. Two Basic Types of Change

> **Gradual change**: Organizational change that is simple and narrowly focused on a specific department or management function, and that has an incremental impact on the hospitality organization.

> **Dynamic change**: Organizational change that is complex and broadly focused and that impacts the entire hospitality organization as it creates a significant difference in its operation.

- Three examples of gradual change:
  - Food trends.
  - Lodging industry competition.
  - Faster/more accurate data collection.

> **Data mining**: The use of technology to analyze guest information in efforts to improve marketing-related decisions.

> **Total quality management (TQM)**: A management system (process) that focuses on identifying what guests want and need, and then consistently delivering these products and services while attaining expected performance standards.

- Three examples of dynamic change

    - New business models.
    - Business expansion.
    - Reorganization.

> **Condo-hotel**: A lodging property that offers transient guest rooms that are owned by persons who place their rooms into the property's rental pool, and who then receive a portion of their room's rental revenues.

- The impact on the total organization, the amount of planning required, the level of employee resistance and the amount of time and effort needed for implementation is likely to increase as the change process moves from gradual to dynamic. The role of human resources in change management, the need for specialized external assistance, the difficulty of reversing the decision, and the costs to implement the change also increase.

b. Role of Human Resources in Change

- The extent of human resources management assistance increases as the organization implements and reacts to intermediate-level change. Total quality management and the expanded use of teams for decision-making purposes require organization-wide communication (top-down but also bottom-up and sideways) to ensure that all possible feedback is available. Training programs that address role-playing, dialog training, brainstorming, and other group decision-making process are necessary.
- When a hospitality organization is confronted with dynamic change, it can become a significant challenge to continue day-to-day operations. Managers at higher organization levels will be involved with numerous planning activities and with implementation tactics driven by their plans.
- Determining reporting relationships so organizational charts can be revised, working with higher-level managers to develop job descriptions, planning recruitment activities, and participating in selection decisions are examples of tasks that become important at this time. If new staff members, including specialists, must be employed as part of efforts to implement dynamic change, still more human resources responsibilities become evident.

4. Resistance to Organizational Change

- One common concern relates to honest differences of opinion about the factor(s) suggesting the need for a change (or if there is even the need for a change) and the best approach to address the change.

> **Brainstorm**: A decision-making approach in which group members suggest alternative potential causes and/or solutions to problems for group consideration.

- Reasons why good employees may resist change:

  - Concerns about the change or the change process.

Human Resources Tactics

Communicate (explain, defend, justify) the need for the change; indicate benefits to the affected staff members; solicit input from employees as changes are planned and implemented.

  - Uncertainty about one's professional future.

Human Resources Tactics

An ongoing relationship of trust and respect (which those with human resources responsibilities must earn) and the nurture of a corporate culture emphasizing high ethical standards will help satisfy employees who may wonder about any hidden agendas that prompt change. Managers who indicate that changes are needed and existing staff are important in their implementation will be believed when they have established a relationship of trust.

  - Conflict between organizational levels.

Human Resources Tactics

Communication is the key. Human resources personnel should be at the same organizational level as their department head counterparts. Their role in developing and implementing equitable policies and procedures, along with mutual efforts and agreements during executive committee meetings and at other times, help legitimize, promote, and assist with significant organizational changes.

  - The organization itself.

Human Resources Tactics

The position analysis process with resulting job descriptions that is taught to staff members or that is facilitated by human resources managers can help define roles and develop defensible organizational charts.

  - The organization's culture.

> **Human Resources Tactics**
>
> The manner in which staff members are treated from time of recruitment to ongoing performance evaluation and while being supervised is a direct result of the approaches to human resources management utilized by the organization's leaders.

- Unfamiliarity with change details.

> **Human Resources Tactics**
>
> Communication between managers and their staff members; input from affected personnel as changes are planned, implemented, and evaluated; and the recognition of employee concerns during the change process can be helpful.

Key Terms & Concepts Review: Quiz #1

This key terms and concepts quiz is designed to help you learn and better understand important chapter concepts and improve your Human Resources-related vocabulary.

Match the key terms with their correct definitions.

1. Organizational change _____   a. A general method or plan developed in efforts to attain a long-range goal.

2. Niche marketing _____   b. A specific action step used to help attain a short-term objective.

3. Strategy _____   c. A systematic method of developing long-term plans to attain business objectives by anticipating and adapting to expected changes.

4. Tactic _____   d. Strengths, Weaknesses, Opportunities, and Threats Analysis—a systematic approach to assess an organization's current environment as part of the strategic planning process.

5. Strategic planning _____   e. A plan in which the final year in the planning cycle is moved ahead one year as plans for each year are implemented.

6. SWOT analysis _____   f. The activity of offering specific products and services to sub segments of a market in efforts to attract large numbers of this sub segment to the operation.

7. Rolling plan (long-range planning) _____   g. The process by which an organization moves away from what it is currently doing toward some desirable future status.

Key Terms & Concepts Review: Quiz #2

This key terms and concepts quiz is designed to help you learn and better understand important chapter concepts and improve your Human Resources-related vocabulary. Match the key terms with their correct definitions.

1. Gradual change _____

    a.   The use of technology to analyze guest information in efforts to improve marketing-related decisions.

2. Dynamic change _____

    b.   A decision-making approach in which group members suggest alternative potential causes and/or solutions to problems for group consideration

3. Data mining: _____

    c.   A lodging property that offers transient guest rooms that are owned by persons who place their rooms into the property's rental pool, and who then receive a portion of their room's rental revenues.

4. Total quality management (TQM) _____

    d.   Organizational change that is complex and broadly focused and that impacts the entire hospitality organization as it creates a significant difference in its operation.

5. Condo-hotel _____

    e.   Organizational change that is simple and narrowly focused on a specific department or management function, and that has an incremental impact on the hospitality organization

6. Brainstorm _____

    f.   A management system (process) that focuses on identifying what guests want and need, and then consistently delivering these products and services while attaining expected performance standards.

Practice Quiz

To help you test your mastery of the chapter's content, choose the letter of the best answer to each of the questions listed below.

1. The first step in strategic planning is to:
    A. Consider the organization's mission
    B. Scan the environment
    C. Analyze the situation
    D. Identify interim objectives
Page 373

2. Benchmarking and data-gathering procedures are activities most likely to be done in which step of the strategic planning process?
    A. When communicating the plan
    B. When identifying interim objectives
    C. When scanning the environment
    D. When determining long-term goals
Page 375

3. When a hospitality organization's newest staff members bring new ideas to the work place, it is an example of:
    A. Dynamic change
    B. Gradual change
    C. Intermediate change
    D. Empowerment
Page 380

4. The following skills must be utilized by a human resource manager when helping their organizations confront and benefit from change:
    A. Business skills
    B. Political skills
    C. People skills
    D. All of the above
Page 388

5. A human resources manager who was busy "scanning the environment" would most likely be involved in which of the following activities:
    A. Disseminating information about the mission statement to staff
    B. Actively participating in community organizations and events
    C. Benchmarking existing work methods
    D. Developing data-mining systems
Page 374

6. Hotels that are specifically designed to attract younger, highly affluent business travelers are an example of:
    A. Data mining
    B. Niche marketing
    C. SWOT analysis
    D. A rolling plan
Page 370

7. The following are all examples of external factors that can influence the need for hospitality organizations to implement changes EXCEPT:
    A. Legislation
    B. Global Issues
    C. Economy
    D. Corporate Culture
Pages 369-370

8. _____ is most helpful to planners attempting to determine the long-term goals of a strategic planning process:
    A. Data mining results
    B. The interim objective
    C. Results of a SWOT analysis
    D. Total quality management
Page 375

9. _____is a specific action step used to help attain a short term goal:
    A. Strategy
    B. Niche
    C. Objective
    D. Tactic
Page 371

10. The plan in which the planning cycle is moved ahead one year as plans for each year are implemented is known as a:
    A. Interim plan
    B. Rolling plan
    C. Business plan
    D. Long-term plan
Page 376

For Your Consideration

In addition to learning about gradual and dynamic change, this chapter introduced you to the concept of anticipated and unanticipated change. Unanticipated change can cause turmoil even in the most experienced of hospitality managers. By their very definition, unanticipated changes catch managers by surprise. Despite that fact, identify three specific unanticipated changes that are "likely" to occur at one time or another in the career of a HR manager working in the hospitality industry and that will affect them on a personal level.

Chapter 12
Critical Issues in Human Resources Management

Learning Objectives Review

At the conclusion of this chapter, you will be able to:

1. Explain how the responsibilities of human resources managers are affected when employees are unionized.

2. Discuss guidelines that are helpful in facilitating the work of staff members belonging to the Traditionalist, Baby Boomer, Generation X, and Generation Y age groups.

3. Provide tactics that may be useful when organizational downsizing and outsourcing strategies are planned and implemented.

4. Review basic procedures that are useful in the succession planning process.

5. Identify the benefits of and basic steps that human resources managers can use to develop and assist staff members with career planning activities.

Study Notes

The following summary includes many of the important points found in this chapter. Key terms are boxed for easy recognition.

1. Unionization in the Hospitality Industry

    a. Reasons for Union Affiliation
    b. A Brief History
    c. The Unionization Process
    d. The Collective Bargaining Process
    e. Contract Administration

> **Unions**: Organizations comprising employees who act together to promote and protect their mutual interests through collective bargaining.

> **Labor contract**: A written agreement covering a specific time that spells out management's expectations for employees and limits to management's authority; also called collective bargaining agreement.

a. Reasons for Union Affiliation

- There are several common reasons why some employees want to unionize. One relates to the employees' perceptions that their employer is unfair and, for example, shows disrespect, disciplines them unjustly, and/or does not correct problems in a reasonable or consistent manner. In other cases, workers believe (rightly or wrongly) that the profits made by the business owners are high, relative to the wages they (the employees) receive, and union affiliation will help spread the profit rewards more equitably.

- Unions can increase the bargaining power of staff members because unified demands on the hospitality organization become possible. Unions also allow members to communicate and interact with higher-level managers in ways that would otherwise be different.

> **Grievance process**: A process to resolve a complaint that is spelled out in union contracts.

> **Union shop**: The requirement that nonunion workers must join the union and pay applicable dues to it.

b. A Brief History

- The historical purpose of labor legislation has been to maintain a balance of power between labor and management. Until the 1930s, unions were discouraged by court rulings as conspiracies in restraint of trade, because there were concerns that employee groups interfered with the right of employers to run their businesses as they desired

- During the Great Depression (1929 throughout most of the 1930s), many politicians began to believe that poor treatment of workers, especially low pay, was a significant factor that contributed to the nation's economic woes. In efforts to achieve a balance of power between labor and management, the National Labor Relations Act (1935), commonly referred to as the Wagner Act, was passed, and it prompted the growth of employee unions in the United States
- The Taft-Hartley Act (1947) amended the Wagner Act and removed some of the power given to unions by that earlier Act. Several unfair labor practices were identified.

> **Union steward**: A union member elected by other union members to represent the unionized employees within a specific department or work unit.

> **Grievance**: An allegation that a work requirement or action taken by management violates the applicable union contract.

> **Seniority**: The status of employees based on their length of employment with an organization.

c. The Unionization Process

- Employees become unionized as the result of a several-step process:
    1. Initial contacts are made by employees to union representatives in their communities or vice versa: union representatives may begin a membership drive within an organization.
    2. A campaign is undertaken to secure signed authorization cards from at least 30 percent of applicable employees requesting that a specific union should represent them in employer negotiations.
    3. After the union has received signed authorization cards, the union or employees can request voluntary recognition of the union. The employer may comply or, alternatively, may request that cards be verified by a neutral third party. If voluntary recognition is granted, contract bargaining can begin.
    4. If the employer refuses voluntary recognition, a petition is made to the National Labor Relations *Board* (NLRB) requesting an election to determine if the majority of eligible voting employees want the union to become their certified bargaining unit.
    5. A union drive is conducted in which union advocates and management must comply with strict requirements about what they can and cannot do as they make their cases about why employees should or should not affiliate with the union.
    6. If the union receives a majority vote, the NLRB certifies and recognizes the union as the exclusive bargaining unit for the employer. As this occurs, there is mandatory recognition.

> **Right-to-work law:** A state law that prohibits a requirement that employees must join a union.

Agency shop: A security arrangement in a labor agreement that requires employees to pay union dues and fees even if they do not join the union.

Open shop: A union security arrangement in which employees are not required to join the union and do not need to pay union dues and fees if they are not union members.

d. The Collective Bargaining Process

Collective bargaining: The process of negotiating and administering written agreements between union and management officials.

Concessions (collective bargaining): The act of conceding (yielding) something as a labor contract is negotiated.

Collective bargaining (distributive): An "I win, you lose" approach to negotiation in which one party attempts to gain something at the expense of the other party.

- Labor contracts typically address concerns that unions make on behalf of their membership. Those that are most typically important relate to compensation, benefits, and job security. Bargaining issues generally concern one of two types. Mandatory items include those about which labor and management must negotiate if either party desires to do so, including wages, working hours, and benefits. Permissible items are those that can be negotiated if labor and management agree to do so (e.g., union veto power over a restaurant's hours of operation).

Collective bargaining (mandatory items): Concerns over which labor and management must negotiate if either party wants to do so.

Collective bargaining (permissible items): Concerns that may be negotiated if both parties agree to do so.

- Three conflict resolution tactics may be used when negotiations reach an impasse:
  - Voluntary arbitration.
  - Compulsory arbitration.
  - Mediation.

e. Contract Administration

- After union and hospitality organization representatives agree to contract provisions, and the contract is ratified (approved) by the union members, communication and coordination efforts are required to ensure that the contract is understood by all parties.
- The union steward represents union employees, and managers represent the organization's interests. They must both consider each other's rights to work together cooperatively.
- Some of the numerous rights that managers should never negotiate away include:
  - Terms and conditions for employee performance reviews
  - The ability to develop schedules that manage overtime
  - Employee assignment, reassignment, and promotion decisions
  - Use of tests to assess employment qualifications
  - Length of probationary periods
  - Expected on-job conduct
  - Discretion to administer work rules, policies, standard operating procedures, and performance standards
  - Modification of job description tasks
  - Implementation of tactics to increase productivity
  - Decisions about staff members qualified for specific positions, merit increases, and promotions
  - Property reorganization including the closure of departments or properties (in multiunit organizations)
- Union agreements affect other aspects of employee relations that should be addressed during orientation, including:
  - Employees' rights and responsibilities
  - Managers' and supervisors' rights and responsibilities
  - Relations with supervisors and union stewards
  - Union contract provisions and company policies
  - Discipline and reprimands
  - Grievance procedures
  - Employment termination

2. A Multigenerational Workforce
a. Overview of the Generations
b. Managing the Generations

a. Overview of the Generations

Traditionalists (workforce generation): Persons with birthdates between approximately 1922 and 1945.

Baby Boomers (workforce generation): Persons with birthdates between approximately 1945 and 1964.

Generation X (workforce generation): Persons with birthdates between approximately 1965 and 1978.

Generation Y (workforce generation): Persons with birthdates between approximately 1979 and 1994.

b. Managing the Generations

- Human resources managers should learn about the generations and their differences because:
    - There are now four generations of employees working side-by-side in the hospitality industry.
    - The industry is labor-intensive and will continue to need employees, regardless of their age, to staff the many available positions.
    - The range of differences between earliest (Traditionalist) employees and the current (Generation Y) staff members is very wide.
    - Differing values, experiences, lifestyles, and attitudes toward the future and life in general can create significant misunderstandings and frustrations.
    - Those who better understand and appreciate each generation may gain ideas about how to motivate and retain persons within these generations, and will be better able to consistently work with individuals of differing ages.

3. Downsizing and Outsourcing
a. Downsizing Tactics
b. Outsourcing Tactics

a. Downsizing Tactics

- Downsizing refers to the process of terminating jobs in efforts to create greater operating efficiencies.

- Some organizations confronted with financial difficulties because of increased costs and/or reduced revenues may need to downsize. Some of their counterparts may desire to proactively eliminate jobs to remain competitive and/or to avoid future problems.
- All downsizing decisions are significant because (1) they impact both the staff members who are terminated and those who remain, and (2) because these decisions affect the organization's financial success and reputation.
- Because the impact of downsizing is difficult to reverse, at least in the short term, several alternatives to the termination of staff members should first be considered depending on the specific challenges confronting the organization. These include:
    - Careful review of alternative opportunities to reduce costs and/or to increase revenues
    - Cross-training
    - Succession planning

    - Transfer within the organization (if a multiunit organization)
    - Reduced employee hours and/or wages
    - Attrition, including the use of early retirement and/or employee buyout incentives and leaves of absence

---

Succession planning: The process of considering the organization's future needs for key professional and other staff, and developing plans to select and/or to prepare persons for these positions.

- As part of the planning process, departmental plans should be developed to help show how each organizational unit will be able to operate effectively after downsizing. Department managers can also be asked to identify work processes that are not needed in the future, so affected positions can be targeted for elimination.

Full-time equivalent: The total number of employees if all employees worked full time, calculated as: total labor hours divided by the average number of labor hours in a workweek. For example, three part-time employees working a total of 45 hours in a workweek represent 1.13 full-time equivalent employees (45 hours ÷ 40 hours) if there are 40 hours in a typical full-time workweek; often abbreviated FTE.

- Those who survive the downsizing effort require special consideration. They must receive ongoing communication from top-level leaders to learn that the separated employees were treated equitably and that they are being helped to find new positions. Other tactics to minimize negative downsizing experiences include:
    - Top-level leaders must be visible and involved, and they must continually re-emphasize the organization's vision, mission, and goals after layoffs are completed.

- Survivors must know where they fit in the reorganized structure and should be given assistance in planning their continued careers with the organization.
- Appropriate rewards and recognition for the remaining employees should be provided.

b. Outsourcing Tactics

Outsourcing: A transfer of responsibility for performance of services that have been (or could be) performed by the organization's employees to an external service provider.

Offshoring: The transfer of jobs from an organization in one country to an organization in another country.

- Priority reasons to consider and implement outsourcing alternatives typically relate to cost concerns and, often, to an inability to attract and retain qualified personnel to perform the necessary work. Some small properties, for example, contract for outside cleaning services. Their service providers employ many staff members and can obtain and provide medical and other benefits at lower costs than can the property using its own employees.

Core business strategies: The highest priority activities that are required to accomplish an organization's mission.

- The process of making an outsourcing decision typically involves the following steps:
    1. Determine exactly what is needed.
    2. Review resources available in-house relative to those available externally.
    3. Identify and evaluate potential bidders.
    4. Develop and issue a Request for Proposal (RFP).
    5. Evaluate proposal responses.
    6. Select a service provider and negotiate the contract.
    7. Administer the service agreement.
    8. Renegotiate or terminate the agreement at its expiration date.

Sarbanes-Oxley Act: The federal government's public company accounting reform and investor protection act that contains numerous provisions focused on improving the accuracy and reliability of corporate disclosures to investors.

---

4. Succession Planning Activities

- Succession planning is a process used by human resources managers to help ensure that they will continue to have the key professional and other staff needed to support their planned growth.
- Steps in succession planning
    - Step 1: Identify priority positions for succession planning.
    - Step 2: Update organizational planning tools.
    - Step 3: Determine the number of position incumbents needed.
    - Step 4: Identify internal staff and/or recruit external staff.
    - Step 5: Plan professional development requirements.
    - Step 6: Develop plans for affected staff.

> **Career**: A sequence of professional experiences and positions in which one participates during a span of employment with an organization or industry.

5. Career Development Programs
   a. Advantages
   b. Procedures for Career Development

> **Career development program**: A planning strategy in which one identifies career goals and then plans education and training activities designed to attain them.

a. Advantages

- Advantages accrue to hospitality organizations that emphasize career development opportunities for their staff, including:

    - Reducing absenteeism and turnover.
    - Assisting with productivity increases.
    - Emphasizing managers' concerns about their staff.
    - Preparing for future challenges.
    - Addressing future labor needs.
    - They allow staff members to learn and gain the experience necessary for promotional opportunities.
    - They help reinforce the employment decisions made by new staff.

b. Procedures of Career Development

- For many persons, career decisions are influenced by factors such as personal interests, likes and dislikes, and being at the right place at the right time. However, a staff member's career plans can also be influenced by opportunities presented by the employer.

- Many staff members will not require significant encouragement to become involved in professional development programs, but others will. Employees will benefit from their employer's efforts to encourage them to prepare for promotions, and they can do so by participating in well-planned education and training activities.

- Organizations with a culture that allows (encourages) staff members to enjoy what they do provide a win-win situation for all constituencies. Managers in these organizations plan professional development programs to help their staff members become competent in future positions.

Key Terms & Concepts Review: Quiz #1

This key terms and concepts quiz is designed to help you learn and better understand important chapter concepts and improve your Human Resources-related vocabulary.

Match the key terms with their correct definitions.

1. Unions _____
2. Labor contract _____
3. Grievance _____
4. National Labor Relations Board (NLRB) _____
5. Concessions (collective bargaining) _____
6. Collective bargaining (distributive) _____
7. Collective bargaining (integrative) _____
8. Cost-of-living adjustment _____
9. Collective bargaining (mandatory items) _____
10. Collective bargaining (permissible items) _____
11. Arbitration (voluntary) _____

a. An "I win, you win" approach to negotiation in which both parties benefit from the agreement.

b. An organization with responsibility to conduct union representation elections.

c. An arrangement in which future wage increases are tied to the consumer price index that reflects changes in consumer purchasing power.

d. An action in which both parties (organization and union personnel) submit a dispute to an external, disinterested third party for binding or nonbinding resolution after the presentation of evidence and related discussion.

e. Organizations comprising employees who act together to promote and protect their mutual interests through collective bargaining.

f. An allegation that a work requirement or action taken by management violates the applicable union contract.

g. The reduction of staff for the purpose of improving an organization's operating efficiency.

h. Concerns that may be negotiated if both parties agree to do so.

i. An action in which an arbitrator is appointed by the government to make a binding decision on the parties negotiating the contract.

j. The act of conceding (yielding) something as a labor contract is negotiated.

k. Concerns over which labor and management ust negotiate if either party wants to do so.

12. Arbitration
    (compulsory)   _____   l.   A written agreement covering a specific time
                                          that spells out management's expectations for
                                          employees and limits to management's
                                          authority.

13. Downsizing   _____   m.   An "I win, you lose" approach to negotiation
                                          in which one party attempts to gain something
                                          at the expense of the other party.

Key Terms & Concepts Review: Quiz #2

This key terms and concepts quiz is designed to help you learn and better understand important chapter concepts and improve your Human Resources-related vocabulary. Match the key terms with their correct definitions.

1. Succession planning _____
2. Attrition _____
3. Outplacement assistance _____
4. Full-time equivalent _____
5. Survivor (downsizing) _____
6. Outsourcing _____
7. Offshoring _____
8. Core business strategies _____
9. Escape clause _____
10. Request for Proposal _____

a. An employee who is not terminated and who remains with the organization after a downsizing process is completed.

b. The transfer of jobs from an organization in one country to an organization in another country.

c. The process of considering the organization's future needs for key professional and other staff, and developing plans to select and/or to prepare persons for these positions.

d. A transfer of responsibility for performance of services that have been, or could be, performed by the organization's employees to an external service provider.

e. The process of helping employees to secure new employment (e.g., résumé writing assistance, access to necessary equipment, and information about Internet job placement sites).

f. A planning strategy in which one identifies career goals and then plans education and training activities designed to attain them.

g. A document developed by a hospitality organization that requests price quotations for and suggestions and other information about the provision of products and/or services from suppliers deemed eligible to supply them; often abbreviated RFP.

h. A provision in a contract that permits one party to terminate the agreement when one or more specified events occur.

i. The total number of employees if all employees worked full time, calculated as: total labor hours worked divided by the average number of labor hours in a workweek.

j. A sequence of professional experiences and positions in which one participates during a span of employment with an organization or industry.

11. Sarbanes-Oxley Act   _____   k.   The reduction in an organization's workforce because of voluntary or involuntary employee separation.

12. Career   _____   l.   The federal government's public company accounting reform and investor protection act that contains numerous provisions focused on improving the accuracy and reliability of corporate disclosures to investors.

13. Career development program   _____   m.   The highest priority activities that are required to accomplish an organization's mission.

Practice Quiz

To help you test your mastery of the chapter's content, choose the letter of the best answer to each of the questions listed below.

1. The Taft-Hartley Act mandated that unions could no longer:
    A. Strike
    B. Force workers to join the union
    C. Organize more than 100 union employees at a time
    D. Exclude minorities
Page 402

2. _____ is know as the process of negotiating and administering written agreements between union and management officials:
    A. Quid pro quo
    B. Attrition
    C. Collective bargaining
    D. Arbitration
Page 404

3. _____ may be necessary if a compromise cannot be reached and management has to seek advice from a third party to reach an agreement.
    A. Voluntary arbitration
    B. Mediation
    C. Compulsory arbitration
    D. Request for proposal
Page 407

4. All of the following are an alternative to downsizing EXCEPT:
    A. Outplacement assistance
    B. Cross-training
    C. Succession planning
    D. Attrition
Pages 417-418

5. When considering outsourcing, a hospitality organization should be sure to consider the implications of the:
    A. Sarbanes-Oxley Act
    B. Union steward
    C. Right-to-work law
    D. Union security arrangement
Page 425

6. _____ is NOT an example of the responsibilities of a union official:
    A. Negotiating labor contracts
    B. Filing grievances
    C. Approving time off
    D. Calling for work actions
Page 403

7. This generation is considered to be the first "workaholics":
    A. Traditionalists
    B. Generation X
    C. Baby Boomers
    D. Generation Y
Page 413

8. An example of a collective bargaining permissible item would be:
    A. Wages
    B. Working hours
    C. Union veto power over hours of operation
    D. Benefits packages
Page 406

9. As a result of an employer refusing to voluntarily recognize its employees' union, a petition would be sent to:
    A. An OSHA compliance officer
    B. The property manager
    C. The union steward
    D. The National Labor Relations Board
Page 404

10. All of the following are byproducts of a career development program EXCEPT:
    A. Reduce absenteeism and turnover
    B. Increase productivity levels
    C. The addressing of future labor needs
    D. The addition of paid vacation
Page 429-430

For Your Consideration

Historically, only a small proportion of the companies and operations found within the hospitality industry have been unionized. The typical rational given for this fact include factors relate to the work force (for example, that it is highly transient and consists of many part-time workers), or to factors related to the workplace itself (for example, that hospitality units typically are quite small and thus, relatively speaking, employ few workers at each site).

There are, however, a great number of hospitality managers who supervise unionized workers. Explain this seeming contradiction by identifying at least three common settings in which it would be highly likely that the employees supervised by a hospitality manager would belong to an employee union.

Chapter 13
Human Resources: Planning for Global Expansion

Learning Objectives Review

At the conclusion of this chapter, you will be able to:

1. Explain the increased need for hospitality organizations to have a presence in the international marketplace.

2. Review how cultural factors affect the conduct of international business.

3. Discuss the process of and challenges involved in a successful international assignment: selection, preparation, on-job issues, and after-assignment return.

4. Describe important considerations when managing hospitality employees in a foreign country.

Study Notes

The following summary includes many of the important points found in this chapter. Key terms are boxed for easy recognition.

1. Hospitality and Tourism Is a Global Industry

    a. Global Imperative: Why Hospitality Companies Expand Internationally
    b. Stages of Global Expansion
    c. Globalization and Effective Human Resources Management

    a. Global Imperative: Why Hospitality Companies Expand Internationally

- During periods of increasing competition and shrinking market share, hotel chains can grow domestic market share, create new products (brands), and/or expand globally.
- The intense natures of domestic competition and market saturation have prompted restaurant chains to expand globally as well. For example, McDonald's Corporation operates in more than 100 countries. Subway Restaurants has almost 27,000 restaurants in approximately 90 countries. Burger King has more than 200 restaurants in Asia, 350 restaurants throughout Australia and New Zealand, 2,000 units in the European and Middle East regions, and 700 restaurants in Latin

America and the Caribbean. Wendy's International operates more than 3,000 international units.

b. Stages of Global Expansion

- Most hospitality organizations begin to operate and grow domestically. They initially (Stage 1) expand by adding locations in the same or different cities, and then open properties in other states.
- At some point, successful organizations may expand to foreign markets (Stage 2), and basic operating concepts, hopefully modified to meet the needs of the foreign marketplace, are transferred to international locations. However, top-level operating decisions are still typically made in the United States, and top-level managers in global units are generally U.S. expatriates.

- Most hospitality firms that operate internationally negotiate franchising contract or management agreements with individuals or companies in the global location, especially when organizations from developed countries expand to emerging countries (e.g., a U.S.-based company expanding to China).
- Decisions about the mode of entry into another country depend, in part, on the perceptions of executives in expanding organizations about whether trustworthy and qualified investors are available locally.

Mode of entry: The process by which a hospitality organization begins a business in another country.

- As hospitality organizations evolve to Stage 3, the organization may collaborate with a host country, organizations, and/or individuals, and foreign divisions, subsidiaries, or joint ventures may develop.

Subsidiaries: A foreign company operated by a domestic hospitality organization with majority (more than 50 percent) ownership by another (parent) company.

Joint venture: A foreign branch partially owned by the domestic organization and partially owned by an entity in the host (foreign) country. Ownership could be a company, several companies, one or more individuals, and/or the government.

- Hospitality operations become multinational (Stage 4) in scope when they expand to several (or more) countries and regions throughout the world. Hospitality operations become multinational (Stage 4) in scope when they expand to several (or more) countries and regions throughout the world.

> **Multinational (organization)**: A hospitality organization with operating units in many countries and regions of the world.

- Finally (in Stage 5), organizations become transnational in scope. Highly decentralized governing boards comprise people from different countries, and staff members from anywhere in the world may be recruited for positions at all, including the highest, organizational levels.

> **Transnational (organization)**: A company with operations throughout the world that features highly decentralized decision making, is less aligned with its country of origin, and that may have weak ties to any specific country.

c. Globalization and Effective Human Resources Management

- Today, many observers believe that the globalization of markets and production has reached a tipping point in which the world economy has moved from self-contained entities to an interdependent global economic system.

- As hospitality corporations grow internationally and, as individuals increasingly work across borders in this interdependent global arena, organizations must conceptualize and implement human resource practices to remain effective.

- Effective hospitality managers working on a domestic or international assignment must recognize the influence of a person's culture and consider and modify management and supervisory tactics accordingly.

- Hospitality operators are increasingly dependent on the political actions, economies, and other influences that affect countries throughout the world marketplace. This is of obvious importance in the hotel industry, which enjoys high or suffers through low occupancy periods based on economic conditions.

- Global influences, then, are an important concern to hospitality managers, because they influence the number of guests who come through their doors.

2. Cultural Factors Impact International Operations

    a. Cultural Concerns Are Important
    b. Cultural Dimensions Impact Hospitality Operations

a. Cultural Concerns Are Important

- The thoughts, words, and actions of employees are typically affected, in part, by their culture: the collective programming of common beliefs, values, behaviors, and other factors that influence what an individual believes and how a person acts.

Culture: A set of learned beliefs, values, and behaviors that influence the way of life shared by the members of a society.

Organizational culture: A set of understandings shared by members of an organization that are relevant and distinctive, that are passed on to new group members, and that influence organizational decision making.

- Managers should anticipate likely responses and incorporate their knowledge of cultural differences into the way they facilitate work. At the same time, they must realize that this knowledge must be modified for the specific situation.

Sociocultural: Relating to social and cultural matters.

- Communication issues should also be addressed in the hospitality workplace. Many nations (including the United States) have vast numbers of people who speak different languages.

- Human resources policies affecting holidays, sex discrimination, job advancement, retirement, work breaks, and employee selection (among many others) can be influenced by religious factors that are integral to the dominant culture in many locations.

b. Cultural Dimensions Impact Hospitality Operations

Country cluster: The notion that some countries can be grouped together based on their population's characteristics, such as language, location, ethnicity, religion, and economic status.

- Hofstede's five cultural dimensions are:
    1. Power distance.
    2. Individualism.
    3. Risk avoidance.
    4. Rigid gender roles.
    5. Past, present, and future orientation.

- While one cannot stereotype all people from a specific culture to fit into a specific space on a high-value to low-value continuum, it is also ineffective to believe that every person is the same. Successful managers understand basic norms in the culture within which they work, and they use this information to help with human resources decision making.

Cultural intelligence: The process by which one learns about a culture and adjusts thinking and behavior responses when interacting with persons from the culture.

---

3. Focus on International Assignments

    a. Background
    b. Selection Issues
    c. Preparation Activities
    d. On-Job Concerns
    e. After-Assignment Follow-up

a. Background

- Several concerns impact the prospective global candidate professionally and personally, including:
    - The political environment.
    - Economic concerns.
    - Cultural environment.

Exchange rate: The rate at which the money of one country is exchanged (traded) for that of another country.

Culture shock: The feeling of disorientation and an inability to adjust to a cultural environment that is different from one's own.

- Managers who are likely to have successful expatriate experiences will:
    - Be able to adapt to and accept change.
    - Have an interest in living in another country or region of the world.
    - Know (or have an interest in learning about) the culture and language of the people of the host country.
    - Have the knowledge and skills needed for the assigned job.
    - Be fully supported by their families and, if the family will accompany them, members are equally willing to accept and adapt to the international assignment.

- Have an interest in understanding the perspectives of persons from other cultures.

b. Selection Issues

- A formalized selection process is important. The candidate's experience and ability should be of special concern. Does his or her work experience suit the needs of the position to be filled?

- One who must relocate to help an employer, or who is doing so because it is judged necessary for career advancement, may not have significant positive motivating influences. Other inappropriate reasons for selecting a global assignment include "because it appears exciting," or when perceived problem staff members are relocated to "get them out of the way."

Cross-cultural adaptability: The extent to which a person can be comfortable in a different culture.

---

c. Preparation Activities

- Explanations about how business is conducted within the country of the assignment also become important. This training must also provide details about personal aspects, such as norms of dress, local costs, availability and quality of schools, the local currency, and (seemingly) innumerable other matters involved in adapting to the new environment.

- Much information must be provided to help managers and their families adapt to life in the new country. Examples include:
  - Information about the form of government and the role it plays in business
  - Overview of the prevalent religion(s)
  - Examples of important social and cultural standards
  - Significant information about nonverbal communication
  - Basics of legal concerns that may differ from those in the United States
  - Size, population, history, holidays, recreational activities, and related country-specific information
  - Information about medical facilities and how to access quality medical care
  - Costs for housing, food, and all other likely purchases, and information about currency and exchange rates

d. On-Job Concerns

- Learning about and adapting to the work and the new culture will be continuous during the assignment. For example, numerous fundamental and basic changes in human resources practices will be required from those used in domestic assignments. Those who are properly motivated will find this aspect of the assignment to be enjoyable. By contrast, those who are less prepared may be confronted with the culture shock discussed earlier.

e. After-Assignment Follow-up

- Several concerns (pitfalls) can arise when an expatriate returns from a global assignment:
    - Next assignment.
    - Reverse culture shock.
    - No recognition for global assignment.

Reverse culture shock: Emotional and physiological readjustments that can occur as one returns from an international assignment.

- The after-assignment process is easier if the expatriate has received regular communication and updates from headquarters during the time of the international assignment.

4. Managing Employees During Global Assignments

a. Use Locals or Expatriates?
b. Basic Concerns Are Important
c. Details! Details!

a. Use Locals or Expatriates?

	ADVANTAGES	DISADVANTAGES
USE LOCALS	➤ Lower compensation	➤ Can be a challenge to merge local employment demands with the organization's concerns and needs.
	➤ Increased acceptance of hospitality organization in the community	➤ May be difficult to recruit qualified applicants for vacant positions.
	➤ Easier to incorporate local concerns into the decision-making process	➤ Can reduce the organization's control of labor.
USE EXPATRIATES	➤ Culture is similar to that of the hospitality organization.	➤ Will likely involve significant compensation expenses.
	➤ Closer operating control will be possible.	➤ Makes it more difficult to adapt the organization to the local culture.
	➤ Provides the organization's employees with international management perspectives.	➤ Can have a negative impact on the morale of local employees.
		➤ May need to address government regulations about expatriate employment.

b. Basic Concerns Are Important

- Human resources policies must consider the context within which they will be used, and to do so requires knowledge about the culture of affected staff members.

- Inconsistencies between cultural influences and the policies and procedures will almost certainly be detrimental to the organization's goals. Therefore, training is needed to enable managers without the appropriate background to make effective at-work decisions in many locations around the globe.

c. Details! Details!

- Successful hospitality managers must also know about and utilize numerous details that are driven by culture, custom, precedent, and a long history of how business is conducted.
- Hospitality managers will likely be involved in business meetings and negotiations, and may be responsible for business entertaining. Simple greetings and the giving of gifts are also natural activities in business and personal situations.
- It takes some time to learn about these and other traditions, but successful businesspersons take the time to do so. Then they consistently practice these protocols to enhance their business and off-work relationships with persons from the host country.

Key Terms & Concepts Review: Quiz #1

This key terms and concepts quiz is designed to help you learn and better understand important chapter concepts and improve your Human Resources-related vocabulary.

Match the key terms with their correct definitions.

1. Mode of entry _____

2. Subsidiaries _____

3. Joint venture _____

4. Multinational (organization) _____

5. Transnational (organization) _____

6. Culture _____

7. Organizational culture _____

8. Sociocultural _____

a. A foreign branch partially owned by the domestic organization and partially owned by an entity in the host (foreign) country.

b. A company with operations throughout the world that features highly decentralized decision making, is less aligned with its country of origin, and that may have weak ties to any specific country.

c. A set of learned beliefs, values, and behaviors that influence the way of life shared by the members of a society.

d. Relating to social and cultural matters.

e. The process by which a hospitality organization begins a business in another country.

f. A set of understandings shared by members of an organization that are relevant and distinctive, that are passed on to new group members, and that influence organizational decision making.

g. A hospitality organization with operating units in many countries and regions of the world.

h. A foreign company operated by a domestic hospitality organization with majority (more than 50 percent) ownership by another (parent) company.

Key Terms & Concepts Review: Quiz #2

This key terms and concepts quiz is designed to help you learn and better understand important chapter concepts and improve your Human Resources-related vocabulary. Match the key terms with their correct definitions.

1. Country cluster _____

2. Cultural intelligence _____

3. Exchange rate _____

4. Inflation _____

5. Culture shock _____

6. Cross-cultural adaptability _____

7. Reverse culture shock _____

a. The rate at which the money of one country is exchanged (traded) for that of another country.

b. The feeling of disorientation and an inability to adjust to a cultural environment that is different from one's own.

c. The extent to which a person can be comfortable in a different culture.

d. The notion that some countries can be grouped together based on their population's characteristics, such as language, location, ethnicity, religion, and economic status.

e. Emotional and physiological readjustments that can occur as individuals return from an international assignment.

f. The economic condition that exists when prices charged for products and services increase throughout a country.

g. The process by which one learns about a culture and adjusts thinking and behavior responses when interacting with persons from the culture.

Practice Quiz

To help you test your mastery of the chapter's content, choose the letter of the best answer to each of the questions listed below.

1. This country would most likely be included in the "Nordic" country cluster.
    A. Turkey
    B. Colombia
    C. Sweden
    D. Singapore
Page 450

2. _____ is a characteristic of a culture or organization that places a low value on individualism:
    A. Feedback provided to individual employees
    B. Group-based performance is a reward factor
    C. Belief in individual control and responsibility
    D. Formal systems of control insure compliance with policies
Page 453

3. _____ is a skill that is EXTREEMLY important for an international hospitality manager:
    A. Technical skills
    B. Cultural sensitivity
    C. Functional skills
    D. Stress management
Page 459

4. A mobile expert team who travels to foreign sites on a short-term basis is a:
    A. SWOT team
    B. Virtual alternative team
    C. SWAT team
    D. Empowered team
Page 470

5. Operating with highly decentralized decision making is a feature of a company known as a:
    A. Transnational organization
    B. Subsidiary
    C. Joint venture
    D. Multinational organization
Page 447

6. These countries were the first in which A.S. hotel companies began international expansion:
    A. China and Japan
    B. Germany and France
    C. England and Ireland
    D. Canada and Mexico
Page 442

7. Details about how businesses relations are conducted in foreign countries will likely be observed in:
    A. Length of business meetings
    B. The giving of gifts
    C. Introductory greetings
    D. Both B and C
Page 471

8. When a foreign company is operated by a domestic hospitality organization, but is majority owned by another entity, the company is known as a:
    A. Joint venture
    B. Subsidiary
    C. Multinational organization
    D. Transnational organization
Page 445

9. Management should be prepared to deal with all the following concerns when an expatriate returns from a global assignment EXCEPT:
    A. Reverse culture shock
    B. Educational assistance funds
    C. Their next assignment
    D. Little or no recognition for global assignment
Page 461

10. Global expansion has allowed McDonald's Corporation to operate restaurants in more than _____ countries:
    A. 20
    B. 500
    C. 100
    D. 2,200
Page 442

For Your Consideration

In the U.S., the on-the-job safety and health of hospitality managers is, for the most part, taken for granted. The federal, state and local regulations involving workplace safety are significant, and most managers do not face significant threats to their safety while working. When a hospitality manager's assignment is an international one, however, on-the-job and off-the-job health and safety may not be so easily assumed.

In many European countries (for example, Switzerland, Germany and France) a manager's international assignment would pose few safety and health-related concerns. In some less developed countries, (for example, Nicaragua, Bolivia, the Dominican Republic and others) those concerns may be very real.

Assume you were responsible for making expatriate work assignments for your company and you knew you would be assigning managers to work in a resort located on the beach in a beautiful (but currently under-developed) country. What are the important health and safety-related issues you would want to ensure that you (or the assigned manager) specifically addressed?